ELIZABETH FRY.

ELIZABETH FRY.

BY

MRS. E. R. PITMAN.

236947

GREENWOOD PRESS, PUBLISHERS
NEW YORK

Originally published in 1884
by Roberts Brothers

First Greenwood Printing 1969

Library of Congress Catalogue Card Number 69-14036

PRINTED IN UNITED STATES OF AMERICA

CONTENTS.

CHAPTER I.

ELIZABETH FRY.

CHAPTER I.

A HUNDRED years ago, Norwich was a remarkable centre of religious, social and intellectual life. The presence of officers, quartered
with their troops in the city, and the balls and
festivities which attended the occasional sojourn
of Prince William Frederick, Duke of Gloucester, combined to made the quaint old city
very gay; while the pronounced element of
Quakerism and the refining influences of lit-
erary society permeated the generation of that
day, and its ordinary life, to an extent not easily
conceived in these days of busy locomotion and
new-world travel. Around the institutions of
the established Church had grown up a people
loyal to it, for, as an old cathedral city, the
charm of antiquity attached itself to Norwich;
while Mrs. Opie and others known to literature,
exercised an attraction and stimulus in their

circles, consequent upon the possession of high intellectual powers and good social position. It was in the midst of such surroundings, and with a mind formed by such influences, that Elizabeth Fry, the prison philanthropist and Quaker, grew up to young womanhood.

She was descended from Friends by both parents : her father's family had been followers of the tenets of George Fox for more than a hundred years ; while her mother was grand-daughter of Robert Barclay, the author of the *Apology for the People called Quakers.* It might be supposed that a daughter of Quaker families would have been trained in the strictest adhe-rence to their tenets; but it seems that Mr. and Mrs. John Gurney, Elizabeth's parents, were not "plain Quakers." In other words, they were calm, intellectual, benevolent, courteous and popular people ; not so very unlike others, save that they attended " First-day meeting," but differing from their co-religionists in that they abjured the strict garb and the "thee" and "thou" of those who followed George Fox to unfashionable lengths, whilst their children studied music and dancing. More zealous brethren called the Gurneys "worldly," and shook their heads over their degenerate con-duct ; but, all unseen, Mrs. Gurney was train-ing up her family in ways of usefulness and true wisdom ; while "the fear of the Lord," as the great principle of life and action, was constantly set before them. With such a mother to mould their infant minds and direct their childish understandings, there was not much fear of the younger Gurneys turning out otherwise than well. Those who shook their heads at the "worldliness" of the Gurneys, little dreamt of the remarkable lives which were being moulded under the Gurney roof.

One or two extracts from Mrs. Gurney's diary will afford a fair insight into her character : —

If our piety does not appear adequate to supporting us in the exigencies of life, and I may add, death, surely our hearts cannot be sufficiently devoted to it. Books of controversy on religion are seldom read with profit, not even those in favor of our own particular tenets. The mind stands less in need of conviction than conversion. These reflections have led me to decide on what I most covet for my daughters, as the result of our daily pursuits. As piety is undoubtedly the shortest and securest way to all moral rectitude, young women should be virtuous and good on the broad, firm basis of Christianity; therefore it is not the tenets of any man or sect whatever that are to be inculcated in preference to those rigid but divine truths contained in the New Testament. As it appears to be our reasonable duty to improve our faculties, and by that means to render ourselves useful, it is necessary and very agreeable to be well-informed of our own language, and the Latin as being most permanent, and the French as being the most in general request. The simple beauties of mathematics appear to be so excellent an exercise to the understanding, that they ought on no account to be omitted, and are, perhaps, scarcely less essential than a competent knowledge of ancient and modern history, geography and chronology. To which may be added a knowledge of the most approved branches of natural history, and a capacity of drawing from nature, in order to promote that knowledge and facilitate the pursuit of it. As a great portion of a woman's life ought to be passed in at least regulating the subordinate affairs of a family, she should work plain work herself, neatly; understand the cutting-out of linen; also she should not be ignorant of the common proprieties of a table, or deficient in the economy of any of the most minute affairs of a family. It should be here observed that gentleness of manner is indispensably necessary in women, to say nothing of that polished behavior which adds a charm to every qualification; to both which, it appears pretty certain, children may be led without vanity or affectation by amiable and judicious instruction.

These observations furnish the key-note to Mrs. Gurney's system of training, as well as indicate the strong common-sense and high principles which actuated her. It was small wonder that of her family of twelve children so many of them should rise up to "call her blessed." Neither was it any wonder that Elizabeth, "the dove-like Betsy" of her mother's journal, should idolize that mother with almost passionate devotion.

Elizabeth was born on May 21st, 1780, at

Norwich ; but when she was a child of six years
old, the Gurneys removed to Earlham Hall, a
pleasant ancestral home, about two miles from
the city. The family was an old one, descended
from the Norman lords of Gourney-en-brai, in
Normandy. These Norman lords held lands in
Norfolk, in the time of William Rufus, and have
had, in one line or another, representatives down
to the present day. Some of them, it is recorded,
resided in Somersetshire ; others, the ancestors
of Mrs. Fry, dwelt in Norfolk, generation after
generation, perpetuating the family name and
renown. One of these ancestors, John Gurney,
embraced the principles of George Fox, and
became one of the first members of the Society
of Friends. Thus it came to pass that Quakerism became familiar to her from early childhood — indeed, was hereditary in the family.

Elizabeth tells us that her mother was most
dear to her ; that she seldom left her mother's
side if she could help it, while she would watch
her slumbers with breathless anxiety, fearing
she would never awaken. She also speaks of
suffering much from fear, so that she could not
bear to be left alone in the dark. This nervous
susceptibility followed her for years, although,
with a shyness of disposition and reserve which
was but little understood she refrained from telling her fears. She was considered rather stupid

and dull, and, from being continually described as such, grew neglectful of her studies ; while, at the same time, delicacy of health combined with this natural stupidity to prevent anything like precocious intelligence. Still, Elizabeth was by no means deficient in penetration, tact, or common-sense ; she possessed remarkable insight into character, and exercised her privilege of thinking for herself on most questions. She is described as being a shy, fair child, possessing a poor opinion of herself, and somewhat given to contradiction. She says in her early recollections : "I believe I had not a name only for being obstinate, for my nature had a strong tendency that way, and I was disposed to a spirit of contradiction, always ready to see things a little differently from others, and not willing to yield my sentiments to them."

These traits developed, in all probability, into those which made her so famous in after years. Her faculty for independent investigation, her unswerving loyalty to duty, and her fearless perseverance in works of benevolence, were all foreshadowed in these early days. Add to these characteristics, the religious training which Mrs. Gurney gave her children, the daily reading of the Scriptures, and the quiet ponderings upon the passages read, and we cannot be surprised that such a character was built up in that Quaker home.

At twelve years of age Elizabeth lost her mother, and in consequence suffered much from lack of wise womanly training. The talents she possessed ripened and developed, however, until she became remarkable for originality of thought and action; while the spirit of benevolent enterprise which distinguished her, led her to seek out modes of usefulness not usually practiced by girls. Her obstinacy and spirit of contradiction became in later years gradually merged or transformed into that decision of character, and lady-like firmness, which were so needful to her work, so that obstacles became only incentives to progress, and persecution furnished courage for renewed zeal. Yet all this was tempered with tender, conscientious heart-searching into both motives and actions.

During her "teens" she is described as being tall and slender, peculiarly graceful in the saddle, and fond of dancing. She possessed a pleasing countenance and manner, and grew up to enjoy the occasional parties which she attended with her sisters. Still, from the records of her journal, we find that at this time neither the grave worship of Quakerism nor the gayeties of Norwich satisfied her eager spirit. We find too, how early she kept this journal, and from it we obtain the truest and most interesting glimpses into her character and feelings. Thus at seventeen years of age she wrote : —

I am seventeen to-day. Am I a happier or a better creature than I was this day twelvemonths? I know I am happier—I think I am better. I hope I shall be happier this day year than I am now. I hope to be quite an altered person; to have more knowledge; to have my mind in greater order, and my heart too, that wants to be put in order quite as much. . . . I have seen several things in myself and others I never before remarked, but I have not tried to improve myself—I have given way to my passions, and let them have command over me, I have known my faults and not corrected them—and now I am determined I will once more try with redoubled ardor to overcome my wicked inclinations. I must not flirt; I must not be out of temper with the children; I must not contradict without a cause; I must not allow myself to be angry; I must not exaggerate, which I am inclined to do; I must not give way to luxury; I must not be idle in mind. I must try to give way to every good feeling, and overcome every bad. I have lately been too satirical, so as to hurt sometimes: remember it is always a fault to hurt others.

I have a cross to-night. I had very much set my mind on going to the Oratorio. The Prince is to be there, and by all accounts it will be quite a grand sight, and there will be the finest music; but if my father does not wish me to go, much as I wish it, I will give it up with pleasure, if it be in my power, without a murmur. . . . I went to the Oratorio. I enjoyed it, but I spoke sadly at random—what a bad habit!

There is much difference between being obstinate and steady. If I am bid to do a thing my spirit revolts; if I am asked to do a thing, I am willing. . . . A thought passed my mind that if I had some religion I should be superior to what I am; it would be a bias to better actions. I think I am by degrees losing many excellent qualities.

I am more cross, more proud, more vain, more extravagant. I lay it to my great love of gayety and the world.
I feel, I know I am falling. I do believe if I had a little
true religion I should have a greater support than I have
now; but I have the greatest fear of religion, because I
never saw a person religious who was not enthusiastic.

It will be seen that Elizabeth at this period
enjoyed the musical and social pleasures of Norwich, while at the same time she had decided
leanings towards the plain, religious customs of
the Friends. It is not wonderful that her heart
was in a state of unrest and agitation, that at
times she scarcely knew what she longed for,
nor what she desired to forsake. The society
with which she was accustomed to mingle contained some known in Quaker parlance as "un-
believers"; perhaps in our day they would be
regarded as holding "advanced opinions." One
of the most intimate visitors at Earlham was a
gentleman belonging to the Roman Catholic
communion, but his acquaintance seemed rather
to be a benefit than otherwise, for he referred
the young Gurneys in all matters of faith to the
"written word" rather than to the opinions of
men or books generally. Another visitor, a lady
afterwards known to literature as Mrs. Schimmel-
penninck, was instrumental in leading them to
form sound opinions upon the religious questions of the day. They were thus preserved

from the wave of scepticism which was then sweeping over the society of that day.

Judging from her journal of this date, it is not easy to detect much, if any, promise of the future self-denying philanthropy. She seemed nervously afraid of "enthusiasm in religion"; even sought to shun anything which appeared different from the usual modes of action among the people with whom she mingled. A young girl who confessed that she had "the greatest fear of religion," because in her judgment and experience enthusiasm was always allied with religion, was not, one would suppose, in much danger of becoming remarkable for philanthropy. True, she was accustomed to doing good among the poor and sick, according to her opportunities and station; but this was nothing strange — all the traditions of Quaker life inculcate benevolence and kindly dealing — what she needed was "*the expulsive power of a new affection.*" This "new affection" — the love of Christ — in its turn expelled the worldliness and unrest which existed, and gave a tone to her mental and spiritual nature, which, by steady degrees, lifted her up, and caused her to forget the syren song of earth. Not all at once, — in the story of her newborn earnestness we shall find that the habits and associations of her daily life sometimes acted as drawbacks to her progress in faith. But the seed having once taken root in that youthful heart, germinated, developed, and sprang up, to bear a glorious harvest in the work of reclaiming and uplifting sunken and debased humanity.

CHAPTER II.

THERE was no sharp dividing-line between worldliness and consecration of life in Elizabeth Gurney's case. The work was very gradually accomplished; once started into earnest living, she discerned, what was all unseen before, a path to higher destinies. Standing on the ruins of her former dead self, she strove to attain to higher things. The instrument in this change was a travelling Friend from America — William Savery.

These travelling Friends are deputed, by the Quarterly Meetings to which they belong, to visit and minister among their own body. Their commission is endorsed by the Yearly Meeting of the Ministers and Elders of the Society, before the Friend can extend the journey beyond his own country. The objects of these visits are generally relating to benevolent and philanthropic works, or to the increase of relig-ion among the members of the Society. Joseph John Gurney himself visited America and the

Continent upon similar missions, and in some of his journeys was accompanied by his illustrious sister.

William Savery was expected to address the Meeting of Friends at Norwich, and most, if not all, of the Gurney family were present. Elizabeth had been very remiss in her attendance at meeting; any and every excuse, in addition to her, at times, really delicate health, served to hinder attendance, until her uncle gently but firmly urged the duty upon her. Thenceforward she went a little more frequently, but still was far from being a pattern worshipper; and it will be conceded that few, save spiritual worshippers, could with profit join in the grave silence, or enjoy the equally grave utterances of ordinary meeting. But William Savery was no ordinary man, and the young people at Earlham prepared to listen to him, in case he "felt moved" to speak, with no ordinary attention. Giving an account of this visit, Richenda Gurney admitted that they liked having Yearly Meeting Friends come to preach, for it produced a little change; from the same vivacious pen we have an account of that memorable service. Memorable it was, in that it became the starting-point of a new career to Elizabeth Gurney.

The seven sisters of the Earlham household all sat together during that eventful morning, in

a row, under the gallery. Elizabeth was restless as a rule when at meeting, but something
in the tone of William Savery's voice arrested
her attention, and before he had proceeded very
far she began to weep. She continued to be
agitated until the close of the meeting, when,
making her way to her father, at the men's side
of the house, she requested his permission to
dine at her uncle's. William Savery was a guest
there that day, and, although somewhat surprised at his daughter's desire, Mr. Gurney
consented to the request. To the surprise of
all her friends Elizabeth attended meeting again
in the afternoon, and on her return home in
the carriage her pent-up feelings found vent.
Describing this scene, Richenda Gurney says :
" Betsey sat in the middle and astonished us all
by the great feelings she showed. She wept
most of the way home. The next morning William Savery came to breakfast, and preached to
our dear sister after breakfast, prophesying of
the high and important calling she would be led
into. What she went through in her own mind
I cannot say, but the results were most powerful and most evident. From that day her love
of the world and of pleasure seemed gone."

Her own account of the impressions made
upon her reads just a little quaintly, possibly
because of the unfamiliar Quaker phraseology.

"To-day I have felt that *there is a God!* I have been devotional, and my mind has been led away from the follies that it is mostly wrapped up in. We had much serious conversation ; in short, what he said, and what I felt, was like a refreshing shower falling upon earth that had been dried for ages. It has not made me unhappy ; I have felt ever since *humble.* I have longed for virtue : I hope to be truly virtuous ; to let sophistry fly from my mind ; not to be enthusiastic and foolish but only to be so far religious as will lead to virtue. There seems nothing so little understood as religion."

Good resolutions followed, and determined amendment of life, as far as she conceived this amendment to be in accordance with the Bible. While in this awakened state of mind, a journey to London was projected. Mr. Gurney took her to the metropolis and left her in charge of a trustworthy attendant, in order that she might make full trial of "the world" which she would have to renounce so fully if she embraced plain Quakerism. Among the good resolutions made in view of this journey to London, we find that she determined not to be vain or silly, to be independent of the opinion of others, not to make dress a study, and to read the Bible at all available opportunities. It was perhaps wise in her father to permit this reasoning, philosophi-

cal daughter of his to see the gayeties of London
life before coming to a final decision respecting
taking up the cross of plain Quakerism; but had
her mind been less finely balanced, her judgment
less trained, and her principles less formed, the
result might have been disastrous.

She went, and mingled somewhat freely with
the popular life of the great city. She was
taken to Drury Lane, the Covent Garden
theatres, and to other places of amusement, but
she could not "like plays." She saw some good
actors; witnessed "Hamlet," "Bluebeard," and
other dramas, but confesses that she "cannot
like or enjoy them"; they seemed "so artifi-
cial." Then she somewhat oddly says that
when her hair was dressed "she felt like a mon-
key," and finally concluded that "London was
not the place for heartful pleasure." With her
natural, sound common sense, her discernment,
her intelligence and purity of mind, these
amusements seemed far below the level of those
fitted to satisfy a rational being — so far that she
almost looked down on them with contempt.
The truth was, that having tasted a little of the
purer joy of religion, all other substitutes were
stale and flat, and this although she scarcely
knew enough of the matter to be able correctly
to analyze her own feelings.

Among the persons Elizabeth encountered in

the metropolis, are found mentioned Amelia Opie, Mrs. Siddons, Mrs. Inchbold, "Peter Pindar," and last, but by no means least, the Prince of Wales. Not that she really talked with royalty, but she saw the Prince at the opera; and she tells us that she admired him very much. Indeed, she did not mind owning that she loved grand company, and she certainly enjoyed clever company, for she much relished and appreciated the society of both Mrs. Opie and Mrs. Inchbald. This pre-dilection for high circles and illustrious people was afterwards to bear noble fruit, seeing that she preached often to crowned heads, and princes. But just then she had little idea of the wonderful future which awaited her. She was only trying the experiment as to whether the world, or Christ, were the better master. Deliberately she examined and proved the truth, and with equal deliberation she came to the decision — a decision most remarkable in a girl so young, and so dangerously situ-ated.

Her own review of this period of her life, written thirty years later, sums up the matter more forcibly and calmly than any utterance of a biographer can do. She wrote : —

Here ended this important and interesting visit to Lon-don, where I learned much, and had much to digest. I

saw and entered many scenes of gaiety, many of our
first public places, attended balls and other places of
amusement. I saw many interesting characters in the
world, some of considerable eminence in that day. I
was also cast among the great variety of persons of
different descriptions. I had the high advantage of
attending several most interesting meetings of William
Savery, and having at times his company and that of a
few other friends. It was like the casting die of my
life, however. I believe it was in the ordering of Providence for me, and that the lessons then learnt are to
this day valuable to me. I consider one of the important results was the conviction of those things being
wrong, from seeing them and feeling their effects. I
wholly gave up, on my own ground, attending all public
places of amusement. I saw they tended to promote
evil; therefore, even if I could attend them without being hurt myself, I felt in entering them I lent my aid to
promote that which I was sure, from what I saw, hurt
others, led them from the paths of rectitude, and brought
them into much sin. I felt the vanity and folly of what
are called the pleasures of this life, of which the tendency is not to satisfy, but eventually to enervate and
injure the mind. Those only are real pleasures which
are of an innocent nature, and are used as recreations,
subjected to the Cross of Christ. I was in my judgment much confirmed in the infinite importance of religion as the only real stay, guide, help, comfort in this life,
and the only means of having a hope of partaking of
a better. My understanding was increasingly opened
to receive its truths, although the glad tidings of the
Gospel were very little, if at all, understood by me. I
was like the blind man, although I could hardly be said
to have attained the state of seeing men as trees. I
obtained in this expedition a valuable knowledge of

human nature from the variety I met with; this, I think, was useful to me, though some were very dangerous associates for so young a person, and the way in which I was protected among them is in my remembrance very striking, and leads me to acknowledge that at this most critical period of my life the tender mercy of my God was marvelously displayed towards me, and that His all-powerful — though to me then almost unseen and unknown — hand held me up and protected me.

Self-abnegation and austerity were now to take the place of pleasant frivolities and fashionable amusements. Her conviction was that her mind required the ties and bonds of Quakerism to fit it for immortality. Not that she, in any way, trusted in her own righteousness; for she gives it as her opinion that, while principles of one's own making are useless in the elevation and refinement of character, true religion, on the contrary, does exalt and purify the character. Still the struggle was not over. Long and bitter as it had been, it became still more bitter; and the nightly recurrence of a dream at this period will serve to show how agitated was her mental and spiritual nature. Just emancipated from sceptical principles, accustomed to independent research, and deciding to study the New Testament rather than good books, when on the border-land of indecision and gloomy doubt, yet not wholly convinced or comforted, her sleeping hours reflected the bitter, restless doubt of her waking thoughts. A curious dream followed her almost nightly, and filled her with terror. She imagined herself to be in danger of being washed away by the sea, and as the waves approached her, she experienced all the horror of being drowned. But after she came to the deciding point, or, as she expressed it, "felt that she had really and truly got real faith," she was lifted up in her dream above the waves. Secure upon a rock, above their reach, she watched the water as it tossed and roared, but powerless to hurt her. The dream no more recurred; the struggle was ended, and thankful calm became her portion. She accepted this dream as a lesson that she should not be drowned in the ocean of this world, but should mount above its influence, and remain a faithful and steady servant of God.

Elizabeth's mind turned towards the strict practices of the Friends, as being those most likely to be helpful to her newly-adopted life. A visit paid to some members of the Society at Colebrook Dale, intensified and confirmed those feelings. She says in her journal that it was a dreadful cross to say "thee," and "thou," instead of speaking like other people, and also to adopt the close cap and plain kerchief of the Quakeress; but, in her opinion, it had to be done, or she could not fully renounce the world and serve God. Neither could she hope for thorough appreciation of these things in her beloved home-circle. To be a "plain Quaker," she must in many things be far in advance of father, sisters, and brothers; while in others she must tacitly condemn them. But she was equal to the demand; she counted the cost, and accepted the difficulties. At this time she was about nineteen years of age.

As a beginning, she left off many pleasures such as might have reasonably been considered innocent. For instance, she abandoned her "scarlet riding-habit," she laid aside all personal ornament, and occupied her leisure time in teaching poor children. She commenced a small school for the benefit of the poor children of the city, and in a short time had as many as seventy scholars under her care. How she managed to control and keep quiet so many unruly specimens of humanity, was a standing problem to all who knew her; but it seems not unlikely that those qualities of organization and method which afterwards distinguished her were being trained and developed. Added to these, must be taken into account the power which a strong will always has over weaker minds — an important factor in the matter. Still more must be taken into account the strong, earnest longing of an enthusiastic young soul to benefit those who were living around her. Earnest souls make history. History has great things to tell of men and women of faith ; and Elizabeth Gurney's life-work colored the history of that age. A brief sentence from her journal at this time explains the attitude of her mind towards the outcast, poor, and neglected : " I don't remember ever being at any time with one who was not extremely disgusting, but I felt a sort of love for them, and I do hope I would sacrifice my life for the good of mankind." Very evidently, William Savery's prophesy was coming to pass in the determination of the young Quakeress to do good in her generation.

CHAPTER III.

AFTER a visit in the north of England with her
father and sisters, Elizabeth received proposals
of marriage from Mr. Joseph Fry of London.
His family, also Quakers, were wealthy and of
good position ; but for some time Elizabeth
seemed to hesitate about entering on married
life. Far from looking on marriage as the goal
of her ambition, as is the fashion with many
young women, she was divided in her mind as
to the relative advantages of single and married
life, as they might affect philanthropic and religious work. After consultation with her
friends, however, the offer was accepted, and on
August 19th, 1800, when she was little more
than twenty years of age, she was married to
Mr. Fry, in the Friends' Meeting House, at
Norwich. Very quickly after bidding her
school-children farewell, Mrs. Fry proceeded to
St. Mildred's Court, London, her husband's
place of business, where she commenced to
take up the first duties of wedded life, and
where several of her children were born.

The family into which she married was a
Quaker family of the strictest order. So far
from being singular by her orthodoxy of manners and appearance, she was, in the midst of
the Frys, "the gay, instead of the plain and
scrupulous one of the family." For a little time
she experienced some difficulty in reconciling
her accustomed habits with the straight tenets
of her husband's household and connections,
but in the end succeeded. It seems singular
that one so extremely conscientious as Elizabeth
Fry, should have been considered to fall behind-
hand in that self-denying plainness of act and
speech which characterized others ; but so it
was. And so determined was she to serve God
according to her light, that no mortification of
the flesh was counted too severe provided it
would further the great end she had in view.
Her extreme conscientiousness became manifest
in lesser things ; such, for instance, as anxiety
to keep the strict truth, and that only, in all
kinds of conversation.

Thus, she wrote in her journal :—

I was told by ——— he thought my manners had too
much of the courtier in them, which I know to be the
case, for my disposition leads me to hurt no one that I can
avoid, and I do sometimes but just keep to the truth with
people, from a natural yielding to them in such things as
please them. I think doing so in moderation is pleasant

and useful in society. It is among the things that produce the harmony of society; for the truth must not be
spoken out at all times, at least not the whole truth. Perhaps I am wrong — I do not know if I am — but it will
not always do to tell our minds. . . I am one of those
who try to serve God and Mammon. Now, for instance,
if I wish to say anything I think right to anyone,
I seldom go straight to the point, but mostly by some
softening, round-about way, which, I fear, is very much
from wishing to please man more than his Maker!

It is evident that Elizabeth Fry dared to be
singular ; very possibly only such self-renounc-
ing singularity could have borne such remarkable fruits of philanthropy. It required some
such independent, philosophical character as
hers to strike out a new path for charitable
effort.

During the continuance of the Yearly Meeting in London, the home in St. Mildred's Court
was made a house of entertainment for the
Friends who came from all parts of the country.
It was a curious sight to see the older Friends,
clad in the quaint costume of that age, as they
mingled with the more fashionably or moder-
ately dressed Quakers. The sightseers of London eighty years ago must have looked on
amused at what they considered the vagaries of
those worthy folks. The old Quaker ladies are
described as wearing at that date a close-fitting
white cap, over which was placed a black hood,

and out of doors a low-crowned broad beaver hat. The gowns were neatly made of drab camlet, the waists cut in long peaks, and the skirts hanging in ample folds. For many years past these somewhat antiquated garments have been discarded for sober "coal-scuttles," and silk dresses of black or gray, much to the improvement of the fair wearer's appearance. These Friends were entertained at Mr. Fry's house heartily, and almost religiously. And doubtless many people who were of the "salt of the earth" were numbered among Mr. Fry's guests, while his young wife moved among them the embodiment of refined lady-like hospitality and high principle. Doubtless, too, the quiet home-talk of these worthy folks was only one degree less solemn and sedate than their utterances at Yearly Meeting.

Mrs. Fry followed up her chosen path in ministering to the sick and poor among the slums of London. She visited them at their homes, and traversed dirty courts and uninviting alleys in the quest of individuals needing succor. Sometimes she was made the instrument of blessing; but at other times, like all philanthropists, she was deceived and imposed upon. One day a woman accosted her in the street, asking relief, and holding an infant who was suffering evidently with whooping-cough. Mrs. Fry offered

to go to the woman's house with the intention
of investigating and relieving whatever real
misery may have existed. To her surprise the
mendicant slunk away as if unwilling to be
visited ; but Mrs. Fry was determined to track
her, and at last brought her to earth. The
room — a filthy, dirty, poverty-cursed one —
contained a number of infants in every conceiva-
ble stage of illness and misery. Horror-stricken,
Mrs. Fry requested her own medical attendant
to visit this lazar-house ; but on going thither
next morning he found the woman and her helpless brood of infants gone. It then turned out
that this woman "farmed" infants ; deliberately
neglected them till she succeeded in killing them
off, and then concealed their deaths in order to
continue to receive the wretched pittances
allowed for their maintenance. Such scenes
and facts as these must have opened the eyes of
Mrs. Fry to the condition of the poorest classes
of that day, and educated her in self-denying
labor on their behalf.

She also took an interest in educational matters, and formed an acquaintance with Joseph
Lancaster, the founder of the Monitorial system,
and quickly turned her talents to account in
visiting the workhouse and school belonging to
the Society of Friends at Islington.

About this time, one sister was married to

Mr. Samuel Hoare, and another to Sir Thomas
Fowell Buxton. Other members of her family
passed away from this life; among them her
husband's mother, and a brother's wife. Some
time later Mr. Fry senior, died, and this event
caused the removal of the home from St. Mildred's Court to Plashet, in Essex, the country
seat of the family. Writing of this change, she
said: "I do not think I have ever expressed
the pleasure and comfort I find in a country
life, both for myself and the dear children. It
has frequently led me to feel grateful for the
numerous benefits conferred, and I have also
desired that I may not rest in, nor too much
depend on, any of these outward enjoyments.
It is certainly to me a time of sunshine."

CHAPTER IV.

A COUNTRY HOME.

The delight expressed in her diary upon her removal to Plashet, found vent in efforts to beautify the grounds. The garden-nooks and plantations were filled with wild flowers, gathered by herself and children in seasons of relaxation, and transferred from the coppices, hedgerows and meadows, to the grounds, which appeared to her to be only second in beauty to Earlham. Mrs. Fry was possessed of a keen eye for Nature's beauties. Quick to perceive, and eager to relish the delights of the fair world around, she took pleasure in them, finding relaxation from the many duties which clustered about her in the spot of earth on which her lot was cast. Her journal tells of trials and burdens, and sometimes there peeps out a sentence of regret that the ideal which she had formed of serving God, in the lost years of youth, had been absorbed in "the duties of a careworn wife and mother." Yet what she fancied she had lost in this waiting-time had been gained, after all, in preparation. This quiet, domestic life was not what she had looked forward to when in the first flush of youthful zeal. Still, she was thereby trained to deal with the young and helpless, to enter into sorrows and woes, and to understand and sympathize with quiet suffering. But the time was coming for more active outward service, and when the call came Elizabeth Fry was found ready to obey it.

Towards the end of 1809 her father died, after great suffering; summoned by one of her sisters, Elizabeth hurried down to Earlham to catch, if possible, his parting benediction. She succeeded in arriving soon enough to bear her much-loved parent company during his last few hours of life, and to hear him express, again and again, his confidence in the Saviour, who, in death, was all-sufficient for his needs. As he passed away, her faith and confidence could not forbear expression, and, kneeling at the bedside, she gave utterance to words of thanksgiving for the safe and happy ending of a life which had been so dear to her. The truth was, a burden had been weighing her down for some time past, causing her to question herself most seriously as to whether she were willing to obey "the inward voice" which prompted her to serve God in a certain way.

This specific way was the way of preaching in Meeting, or "bearing testimony," as she phrased it, "at the prompting of the Holy Spirit." It will be remembered that this is a distinguishing peculiarity of the society which George Fox founded. Preaching is only permitted upon the spur of the moment, as people of the world would say, but at the prompting of the inward voice, as Quakers deem. Certainly no one ever became a preacher among the Friends "for a piece of bread." If fanatics sometimes "prophesied" out of the fullness of excited brains, or fervid souls, no place-hunter adopted the pulpit as a profession. Only, sometimes, it needs the presence of an overwhelming trial to bring out the latent strength in a person's nature ; and this trial was furnished to Elizabeth Fry in the shape of her father's death. The thanksgiving uttered by her at his death was also publicly repeated at the funeral, probably with additional words, and from that time she was known as a "minister."

In taking this new departure she must not be confounded with some female orators of the present age, who often succeed in turning preaching into a hideous caricature. She was evidently ripening for her remarkable work, and while doing so was occasionally irresistibly impelled to give utterance to "thoughts that breathe and words that burn." Still, after reaching the quiet of Plashet, and reviewing calmly her new form of service, she thus wrote, what seemed to be both a sincere and common-sense judgment upon herself : —

I was enabled coming along to crave help; in the first place, to be made willing either to do or to suffer whatever was the Divine will concerning me. I also desired that I might not be so occupied with the present state of my mind as to its religious duties, as in any degree to omit close attention to all daily duties, my beloved husband, children, servants, poor, etc. But, if I should be permitted the humiliating path that has appeared to be opening before me, to look well at home, and not discredit the cause I desire to advocate.

Wise counsels these, to herself ! No woman whose judgment is well-balanced, and whose womanly-nature is finely strung, but will regard the path to the rostrum with shrinking and dismay. Either the desire to save and help her fellow-creatures, "plucking them out of the fire," if need be, is so strong upon her as to overmaster all fear of man ; or else the necessities and claims of near and dear ones lay compulsion upon her to win support for them. Therefore, while every woman can be a law unto herself, no woman can be a law unto her sisters in this matter. As proof of her single-ness of heart, another passage may be quoted

from Mrs. Fry's journal. It runs thus, and will
be by no means out of place here, seeing that
it bears particularly upon the new form of ministry then being taken up by her : —

May my being led out of my own family by what
appears to me *duties*, never be permitted to hinder my
doing my duty fully towards it, or so occupy my attention
as to make me in any degree forget or neglect home
duties. I believe it matters not where we are, or what
we are about, so long as we keep our eye fixed on doing
the Great Master's work. . . . . I fear for myself, lest
even this great mercy should prove a temptation, and
lead me to come before I am called, or enter service I
am not prepared for. . . . This matter has been for many
years struggling in my mind, long before I married, and
once or twice when in London I hardly knew how to refrain. However, since a way has thus been made for me
it appears as if I dared not stop the work; if it be a
right one may it go on and prosper, if not, the sooner
stopped the better.

Very soon after penning these words, the
Meeting of which she was a member acknowledged Mrs. Fry as a minister, and thus gave
its sanction to her speaking in their religious
assemblies.

But, not content with this form of service,
she visited among her poor neighbors, bent on
actively doing good. She secured a large room
belonging to an old house, opposite her own
dwelling, and established a school for girls on

2

the Lancasterian pattern there. Very quickly, under the united efforts of Mrs. Fry, the incumbent of the parish, and a benevolent young lady named Powell, a school of seventy girls was established, and kept in a prosperous condition. This school was still in working order a few years ago.

Plashet House was a depot of charity. Calicoes, flannels, jackets, gowns, and pinafores were kept in piles to clothe the naked; drugs suited to domestic practice were stored in a closet, for healing the sick; an amateur soup-kitchen for feeding the hungry was established in a roomy out-building, and this long years before public soup-kitchens became the rage; whilst copies of Testaments were forthcoming on all occasions to teach erring feet the way to Heaven. But her charity did not stop with these things.

An unsavory locality known as "Irish Row," about half a mile off, soon attracted her attention. The slatternliness, suffering, shiftlessness, dirt and raggedness, were inducements to one of her charitable temperament to visit its inhabitants, having their relief and improvement in view; while her appreciation of the warm-heartedness and drollery of the Irish character afforded her genuine pleasure. Proximity to English life had not refined these Irish;

their houses were just as filthy, their windows as patched and obscured with rags, their children just as neglected, and their pigs equally familiar with those children as if they had lived in the wilds of Connemara. Shillalahs, wakes, potatoes, and poverty were distinguishing characteristics of the locality ; whilst its inhabitants were equally ready, with the free and easy volatility of the Irish mind, to raise the jovial song, or utter the cry of distress.

The priest and spiritual director of " Irish Row " found himself almost powerless in the presence of this mass of squalid misery. That Mrs. Fry was a Quaker and a Protestant, did not matter to him, provided she could assist in raising this debased little colony into something like orderly life and decency. So he co-operated with her, and with his consent she gave away Bibles and tracts, vaccinated and taught the children, as well as moved among them generally in the character of their good genius. When delicate and weak, she would take the carriage, filled with blankets and clothes for distribution, down to Irish Row, where the warm-hearted recipients blessed their " Lady bountiful " in terms more voluble and noisy than refined. Still, however unpromising, the soil bore good fruit. Homes grew more civilized, men, women, and children more respectable and quiet, while everywhere the impress of a woman's benevolent labors was apparent.

It was the annual custom of a tribe of gypsies to pitch their tents in a green lane near Plashet, on their way to Fairlop Fair. Once, after the tents were pitched, a child fell ill; the distracted mother applied to the kind lady at Plashet House for relief. Mrs. Fry acceded to the request, and not only ministered to the gypsies that season, but every succeeding year; until she became known and almost worshipped among them. Romany wanderers and Celtic colonists were alike welcome to her heart and purse, and vied in praising her.

About this time the Norwich Auxiliary Bible Society was formed, and Mrs. Fry went down to Earlham to attend the initial meeting. She tells us there were present the Bishop of Norwich, six clergymen of the Established Church, and three dissenting ministers, besides several leading Quakers and gentlemen of the neighborhood. The number included Mr. Hughes, one of the secretaries, and Dr. Steinkopf, a Lutheran minister, who, though as one with the work of the Bible Society, could not speak English. At some of these meetings she felt prompted to speak, and did so at a social gathering at Earlham Hall, when all present owned her remarkable influence upon them. These associations also increased in her that catholic- ity of spirit which afterwards seemed so promi- nent. Some of her brothers and sisters belonged to the Established Church of Eng- land ; while in her walks of mercy she was con- tinually co-operating with members of other sections of Christians. As we have seen, she worked harmoniously with all : Catholic and Protestant, Churchman and Dissenter.

On looking at her training for her special form of usefulness we find that afflictions pre- dominated just when her mind was soaring above the social and conventional trammels which at one time weighed so much with her. We know her mostly as a prison philanthropist; but while following her career in that path, it will be wise not to forget the way in which she was led. By slow and painful degrees she was drawn away from the circles of fashion in which once her soul delighted. Then her nature seemed so retiring, and the tone of her piety so mystical, while she dreaded nervously all approach to " religious enthusiasm," that a career of publicity, either in prisons, among rulers, or among the ministers of her own Soci- ety, seemed too far away to be ever realized in fact and deed. Only He, who weighs thoughts and searches out spirits, knew or understood by what slow degrees she rose to the demands which presented themselves to her "in the ways of His requirings," even if "they led her into suffering and death." It was no small cross for such a woman thus to dare singularity and possibly odium.

CHAPTER V.

It is said by some authorities that in her childhood Mrs. Fry expressed so great a desire to
visit a prison that her father at last took her to
see one. Early in 1813 she first visited Newgate,
with the view of ministering to the necessities
of the felons ; and for all practical purposes of
charity this was really her initial step. The following entry in her journal relates to a visit paid
in February of that year. " Yesterday we were
some hours with the poor female felons, attending to their outward necessities ; we had been
twice previously. Before we went away dear
Anna Buxton uttered a few words of supplication, and, very unexpectedly to myself, I did
also. I' heard weeping, and I thought they
appeared much tendered (*i. e.* softened) ; a very
solemn quiet was observed ; it was a striking
scene, the poor people on their knees around us
in their deplorable condition." This reference
makes no mention of what was really the truth,
that some members of the Society of Friends,

who had visited Newgate in January, had so
represented the condition of the prisoners to
Mrs. Fry that she determined to set out in this
new path. " In prison, and ye visited me."
Little did she dream on what a distinguished
career of philanthropy she was entering.

And Newgate needed some apostle of mercy
to reduce the sum of human misery found there,
to something like endurable proportions. We
are told that at that date all the female prisoners were confined in what was afterwards known
as the " untried side" of the jail, while the larger
portion of the quadrangle was utilized as a state-
prison. The women's division consisted of two
wards and two cells, containing a superficial
area of about one hundred and ninety yards.
Into these apartments, at the time of Mrs. Fry's
visit, above three hundred women were crammed,
innocent and guilty, tried and untried, misde-
meanants, and those who were soon to pay the
penalty of their crimes upon the gallows.
Besides all these were to be found numerous
children, the offspring of the wretched women,
learning vice and defilement from the very cradle. The penal laws were so sanguinary that at
the commencement of this century about three
hundred crimes were punishable with death.
Some of these offences were very trivial, such
as robbing hen-roosts, writing threatening let-

ters, and stealing property from the person to
the amount of five shillings. There was always
a good crop for the gallows: hanging went mer-
rily on, from assize town to assize town, until one
wonders whether the people were not gallows-
hardened. One old man and his son performed
the duties of warders in this filthy, abominable
hole of "justice." And the ragged, wretched
crew bemoaned their wretchedness in vain, for
no helping hand was held out to succor. They
were "destitute of sufficient clothing, for which
there was no provision ; in rags and dirt, without bedding, they slept on the floor, the boards
of which were in part raised to supply a sort of
pillow. In the same rooms they lived, cooked,
and washed. With the proceeds of their clam-
orous begging, when any stranger appeared
among them, the prisoners purchased liquors
from a tap in the prison. Spirits were openly
drunk, and the ear was assailed by the most
terrible language. Beyond the necessity for
safe custody, there was little restraint upon
their communication with the world without.
Although military sentinels were posted on the
leads of the prison, such was the lawlessness
prevailing, that Mr. Newman, the governor,
entered this portion of it with reluctance."

As Mrs. Fry and the "Anna Buxton" referred to, — who was a sister of Sir Thomas

Fowell Buxton, — were about to enter this modern Inferno, the Governor of Newgate advised
the ladies to leave their watches in his care lest
they should be snatched away by the lawless
wretches inside. But no such hesitating, half-
hearted, fearful charity was theirs. They had
come to see for themselves the misery which
prevailed, and to dare all risks ; and we do not
find that either Mrs. Fry or her companion lost
anything in their progress through the women's
wards ; watches and all came away safely, a
fresh proof of the power of kindness. The
revelations of the terrible woes of felon-life
which met Mrs. Fry stirred up her soul within
her. She emphatically "clothed the naked,"
for she set her family to work at once making
green-baize garments for this purpose until she
had provided for all the most destitute.

To remedy this state of things appeared like
one of the labors of Hercules. Few were hopeful of the success of her undertaking, while at
times even her undaunted spirit must have
doubted. In John Howard's time the prisons
of England had been distinguished for vice,
filth, brutality, and suffering ; and although
some little improvement had taken place, it
was. almost infinitesimal. Old castles, or gate-
houses, with damp, dark dungeons and narrow
cells, were utilized for penal purposes. It was

common to see a box fastened up under one of the narrow, iron-barred windows overlooking the street, with the inscription, " Pity the poor prisoners," the alms being intended for their relief and sustenance. Often the jail was upon a bridge at the entrance of a town, and the damp of the river added to the otherwise unhealthy condition of the place. Bunyan spoke, not altogether allegorically, but rather literally, of the foul " den " in which he passed a good twelve years of his life. Irons and fetters were used to prevent escape, while those who could not obtain the means of subsistence from their friends, suffered the horrors of starvation. Over-crowding, disease, riot, and obscenity united to render these places very Pandemoniums.

It seemed almost hopeless to deal with ferocious and abandoned women. One of them was observed, desperate with rage, tearing the caps from the heads of the other women, and yelling like a savage beast. By so much nearer as woman is to the angels, must be measured her descent into ruin when she is degraded. She falls deeper than a man ; her degradation is more complete, her nature more demoralized. Whether Mrs. Fry felt unequal just then to the task, or whether family affliction pressed too sorely upon her, we do not

know; her journal affords no solution of the
problem, but certain it is that some three years
passed by before any very active steps were
taken by her to ameliorate to any decided
extent the misery of the prisoners.

But the matter seethed in her mind; as she
mused upon it, the fire burned, and the spirit
which had to burst its conventional trammels
and "take up the cross" in regard to dress and
speech, looked out for other crosses to carry.
Doing good became a passion; want, misery,
sin and sorrow furnished claims upon her which
she would neither ignore nor deny.

John Howard had grappled with the hydra
before her, and finally succumbed to his exertions. As the period of his labors lay principally between the years 1774 and 1790, when
the evils against which Mrs. Fry had to contend
were intensified and a hundred times blacker, it
cannot do harm to recall the condition of prisons
in England during the last quarter of the
eighteenth century; that is, during the girlhood
of Elizabeth Fry. Possibly some echoes of the
marvellous exertions of Howard in prison reform had reached her Earlham home, and produced, though unconsciously, an interest in the
subject which was destined to bear fruit at a
later period. At any rate, the fact cannot be
gainsaid that she followed in his steps, visiting

the Continent in the prosecution of her self-imposed task, and examining into the most loathsome recesses of prisons, lunatic asylums, and hospitals.

The penal systems of England had been on their trial; had broken down, and been found utterly wanting. Modern legislation and phil-anthropy have laid it down that *reform* is the proper end of all punishment; hence the "silent system," the "separate system," and various employments have been adopted. Hence, too, arose the framing of a system of education and instruction under the jail roof, so that on the discharge of prisoners they might be fitted to earn their own maintenance in that world which formerly they had cursed with their evil deeds. But it was not so in the era of John Howard, nor of Elizabeth Fry. Then, justice made short work with criminals and debtors. The former it hanged in droves, and left the latter to liter-ally "rot" in prison. Two systems of transpor-tation have been tried: the one previous to Howard's day succeeded in pouring into the American plantations the crime and vice of England; whilst the other, which succeeded him, did the same for Australia. After the breach between the American colonies and the mother-country, the system of transportation to the Transatlantic plantations ceased; it was in the succeeding years that the foul holes called prisons, killed their thousands, and "jail-fever" its tens of thousands.

Yet, in spite of hanging felons faster than any other nation in Europe, in spite of killing them off slowly by the miseries of these holes, crime multiplied more than ever. Gigantic social corruptions festered in the midst of the nation, until it seemed as if a war which carried off a few thousands or tens of thousands of the lower classes, were almost a blessing. Alongside the horrible evils for which Government was responsible, grew up multitudes of other evils against which it fought, or over which it exercised a strong and somewhat tyrannical upper-hand. In society there was a constant war going on between law and crime. Extirpation — not reform — was the end aimed at ; the prison officials of that time looked upon a criminal as a helpless wretch, presenting fair game for plunder, torture and tyranny. The records in Howard's journals, and the annals of Mrs. Fry's labors, amply enlighten us as to the result of this state of things.

In Bedford jail the dungeons for felons were eleven feet below the ground, always wet and slimy, and upon these floors the inmates had to sleep. At Nottingham the jail stood on the side of a hill, while the dungeons were cut in

the solid rock; these dungeons could only be
entered after descending more than thirty steps.
At Gloucester there was but one court for all
prisoners, and, while fever was decimating
them, only one day-room. At Salisbury the
prisoners were chained together at Christmas
time and sent in couples to beg. In some of
the jails, open sewers ran through corridors and
cells, so that the poor inmates had to fight for
their lives with the vermin which flourished
there. At Ely the prison was in such a ruinous condition that the criminals could not be
safely kept; the warders, therefore, had had
recourse to chains and fetters to prevent the
escape of those committed to their charge.
They chained prisoners on their backs to the
floor, and, not content with this, secured iron
collars round their necks as well as placed heavy
bars across their legs. Small fear of the poor
wretches running away after that! At Exeter
the county jail was the private property of a
gentleman, John Denny Rolle, who farmed it
out to a keeper, and received an income of
twenty pounds per annum for it. Yet why mul-
tiply instances! In all of them, dirt, cruelty,
fever, torture and abuses reigned unchecked.
Prisoners had no regular allowance of food, but
depended on their means, family, or charity;
the prisons were farmed by their keepers, some

of whom were women, but degraded and cruel;
many innocent prisoners were slowly rotting to
death, because of their inability to pay the
heavy fees exacted by their keepers ; while the
sleeping-rooms were so crowded at times, that
it was impossible for the prisoners to lie down
all together for sheer lack of space. Torture
was prohibited by the law of England, but
many inhuman keepers used thumb-screws and
iron caps with obnoxious prisoners, for the
amusement of themselves and their boon companions. Several cases of this kind are recorded.

So hideous an outcry arose against these horrors, that at last Parliament interfered, and
passed two bills dealing with prisoners and
their treatment. The first of these provided
that when a prisoner was discharged for want
of prosecution he should be immediately set
free, without being called upon to defray any
fees claimed by the jailer or sheriff ; while the
second bill authorized justices of the peace to
see to the maintenance of cleanliness in the prisons. The first set at liberty hundreds of innocent persons who were still bound because they
could not meet the ruinous fees demanded from
them; while the second undoubtedly saved the
lives of hundreds more. These were instal-
ments of reform.

Thus it will easily be understood that whatever the condition of Newgate and other English prisons was, at the date of Mrs. Fry's
labors, they were far better than in previous
years. Some attempts had been made to render these pest-houses less horrible; but for
lack of wise, intelligent management, and occupation for the prisoners, the wards still presented pictures of Pandemonium. It needed a
second reformer to take up the work where
Howard left it, and to labor on behalf of the
convicts; for in too many cases they were
looked upon as possessing neither right nor
place on God's earth. In the olden days, some
judges had publicly declared their preference
for hanging, because the criminal would then
trouble neither State nor society any further.
But in spite of Tyburn horrors, each week
society furnished fresh wretches for the gallows; whilst those who were in custody were
almost regarded as "fore-doomed and fore-
damned."

During the interval which elapsed between
Mrs. Fry's short visits to Newgate in 1813, and
the resumption of those visits in 1817, together
with the inauguration of her special work among
the convicts, she was placed in the crucible of
trial. Death claimed several relatives; she suffered long-continued illness, and experienced

considerable losses of property. All these things refined the gold of her character and discovered its sterling worth. Some natures grow hard and sullen under trial, others faithless and desponding, and yet others narrow and reserved. But the genuine gold of a noble disposition comes out brighter and purer because of untoward events ; unsuspected resources are developed, and the higher nobility becomes discernable. So it was with Elizabeth Fry. The constitutional timidity of her nature vanished before the overpowering sense of duty ; and literally she looked not at the seen, but at the unseen, in her calculations of Christian service. Yet another part of her discipline was the ingratitude with which many of her efforts were met. This experience is common to all who labor for the public weal ; and from an entry in her journal we can but conclude that this " serpent's tooth " pierced her very sorely at times. "A constant lesson to myself is the ingratitude and discontent which I see in many." Many a reformer could echo these words. But the abiding trial seemed to be the remembrance of the loss of her little daughter, Elizabeth, who passed away after a week of suffering, and who was laid to rest in Barking churchyard. The memory of this five-year old child remained with her for many years a pure and holy influence,

doubtless prompting her to deal tenderly with
the young strayed ones whom she met in her
errands of mercy. How often the memory of
" the touch of a vanished hand, and the sound
of a voice that is still," influences our intercourse with the living, so that while benefiting
them we do it as unto and for the dead.

CHAPTER VI.

NEWGATE HORRORS AND NEWGATE WORKERS.

ABOUT Christmas 1816, or January 1817, Mrs. Fry commenced her leviathan task in good earnest. The world had been full of startling events since her first two or three tentative visits to Newgate; so startling were they, that even in the refined and sedate quietude of Quakerism there must have existed intense interest, excitement, and possibly fear. We know from Isaac Taylor's prolific pen, how absorbing was the idea of invasion by the French, how real a terror was Bonaparte, and how full of menace the political horizon appeared. Empires were rising and falling, wars and tumults were the normal condition of society; the Continent was in a state of agitation and warfare. Napoleon, the prisoner of Elba, had returned to Europe, collected an army, and, contesting at Waterloo the strength of England and Prussia, had fallen. He was now watched and guarded at St. Helena, while the civilized world began to breathe freely. The mushroom kingdoms which he had set up were fast tottering, or had fallen, while the older dynasties of Europe were feeling once more secure, because the man who hesitated not to sacrifice vast myriads of human lives to accomplish his own aggrandizement, was now bound, and, like a tiger in chains, could do nought save growl impotently.

Meanwhile the tide of prison-life went on without much variation. Newgate horrors still continued ; the gallows-crop never failed ; and the few Acts of Parliament designed to ameliorate the condition of the prisoners in the jails had almost become dead letters. In 1815 a deputation of the Jail Committee of the Corporation of London visited several jails in order to examine into their condition, and to introduce a little improvement, if possible, into those under their care. This step led to some alterations ; the sexes were separated, and the women were provided with mats to sleep upon. Visitors were restrained from having much communication with the prisoners, a double row of gratings being placed between the criminals and those who came to see them. Across the space between the gratings it was a common practice for the prisoners to push wooden spoons, fastened to long sticks, in order to receive the contributions of friends. Disgusting in its ways, vicious in act and speech, the social scum which crowded Newgate was repulsive, dangerous, and vile in the extreme.

It is evident that the circle to which Mrs. Fry belonged was still interested, in philanthropic labors on behalf of the criminal classes, because we find that Sir Thomas F. Buxton, Mr. Hoare, and several other friends were busy, in the interval between 1813 and 1816, in establishing a society for the reformation of juvenile thieves. This matter of prison discipline was therefore engaging the attention of her immediate circle. Doubtless, while listening to them, she remembered most anxiously the miserable women whom she had visited some three years previously.

It seems that Mrs. Fry succeeded with the women by means of her care for the children. Low as they were in sin, every spark of maternal affection had not fled, and they craved for their little ones a better chance than they had possessed themselves. To a suggestion by Mrs. Fry that a school should be formed for the benefit of their little ones they eagerly acceded. This suggestion she left with them for consideration, engaging to come to a decision at the next visit.

At the next visit she found that the tears of joy with which they had welcomed the proposition were not feigned. The women had already

chosen a school-mistress from among themselves. A young woman, named Mary Cormer,
who had, although fairly educated, found her
way to prison for stealing a watch, was the person chosen. It is recorded of this young woman
that she became reformed during her stay in
Newgate, and so exemplary did she behave in
the character of teacher, that Government
granted her a free pardon ; which, however, she
did not live long to enjoy.

It is pleasant to record that the officials aided
and furthered this good work. An empty cell
was granted for the school-room, and was quickly crammed with the youngest of the criminals.
After this step had been taken, a young Friend
named Mary Sanderson made her appearance at
Newgate to assist, if it were possible, in the
work, but was almost terrified away again. She
informed Sir Thomas Fowell Buxton of her experiences and terrors at her first encounter with
the women : "The railing was crowded with
half-naked women, struggling together for the
front situations with the most boisterous violence, and begging with the utmost vocifera-
tion." She felt as if she were going into a den
of wild beasts, and she well recollects quite
shuddering when the door was closed upon her,
and she was locked in with such a herd of novel
and desperate companions.

Could lasting good be effected there? It seemed hopeless. Indeed, at first it was scarcely dreamt of; but, the stone once set rolling, none knew where it would stop. Marvellous to say, some of the prisoners themselves asked for ministrations of this sort. Feeling that they were as low down in the mire as they could be, they craved a helping hand; indeed, entreated not to be left out from the benevolent operations which Mrs. Fry now commenced. The officers of Newgate despaired of any good result; the people who associated with Mrs. Fry, charitable as they were, viewed her plans as Utopian and visionary, while she herself almost quailed at their very contemplation. It also placed a great strain upon her nervous system to attend women condemned to death. She wrote: "I have suffered much about the hanging of criminals." And again: "I have just returned from a melancholy visit to Newgate, where I have been at the request of Elizabeth Fricker, previous to her execution to-morrow at 8 o'clock. I found her much hurried, distressed and tormented in mind. Her hands were cold, and covered with something like the perspiration which precedes death, and in an universal tremor. The women who were with her said she had been so outrageous before our going, that they thought a man must be sent for to manage her. However, after a serious time with her, her troubled soul became calmed." Another entry in the same journal casts a lurid light upon the interior of Newgate. "Besides this poor young woman, there are also six men to be hanged, one of whom has a wife near her confinement, also condemned, and seven young children. Since the awful report came down he has become quite mad from horror of mind. A straight waistcoat could not keep him within bounds ; he had just bitten the turnkey ; I saw the man come out with his hand bleeding as I passed the cell. I hear that another who has been tolerably educated and brought up, was doing all he could to harden himself through unbelief, trying to convince himself that relig-ous truths were idle tales." Contemporary light is cast upon this matter by a letter which the Hon. G. H. Bennett addressed to the Cor-poration of London, relative to the condition of the prison. In it this writer observed : —

A man by the name of Kelly, who was executed some weeks back for robbing a house, counteracted, by his conversation and by the jests he made of all religious subjects, the labors of Dr. Cotton to produce repentance and remorse among the prisoners in the cells; and he died as he lived, hardened and unrepenting. He sent to me the day before his execution, and when I saw him *he maintained the innocence of the woman convicted with him* (Fricker, before mentioned), asserting that not her,

but a boy concealed, opened the door and let him into
the house. When I pressed him to tell me the names
of the parties concerned, whereby to save the woman's
life, he declined complying without promise of a pardon.
I urged as strongly as I could the crime of suffering an
innocent woman to be executed to screen criminal
accomplices; but it was all to no effect, and he suffered,
maintaining to the last the same story.· With him was
executed a lad of nineteen or twenty years of age, whose
fears and remorse Kelly was constantly ridiculing.

About this time, Mrs. Fry noted in her journal the encouragement she had received from
those who were in authority, as well as the
eager and thankful attitude of the poor women
themselves. Kindred spirits were being drawn
around her, ready to participate in her labors of
love. In one place she wrote almost deprecat-
ingly of the publicity which those labors had
won ; she feared notoriety, and would, had it
been possible, have worked on alone and un-
heralded. But perhaps it was as well that
others should learn to coöperate ; the task was
far too mighty for one frail pair of hands, while
the increased knowledge and interest among
the upper classes of society assisted in procuring the "sinews of war." For this was a work
which could not be successfully carried on without pounds, shillings and pence. Clothing,
books, teachers, and even officers had to be
paid for out of benevolent funds, for not an

idea of the necessity for such funds had ever crossed the civic mind.

A very cheering item, in April, 1817, was the formation of a ladies' society under the title of "An Association for the Improvement of the Female Prisoners in Newgate." Eleven Qua-keresses and one clergyman's wife were then banded together. We cannot find the names of these good women recorded anywhere in Mrs. Fry's journal. The object of this associa-tion was : "To provide for the clothing, instruc-tion, and employment of the women ; to intro-duce them to a knowledge of the Scriptures, and to form in them, as much as possible, those habits of sobriety, order and industry, which may render them docile and peaceable whilst in prison, and respectable when they leave it." Thus, stone by stone the edifice was being reared, step by step was gained, and everything was steadily advancing towards success. The magistrates and corporation of the city were favorable, and even hopeful ; the jail officials were not unwilling to coöperate, and ladies were anxious to take up the work. The last thing which remained was to get the assent and willing submission of the prisoners themselves to the rules which *must* be enforced, were any lasting benefit to be conferred ; and to this last step Mrs. Fry was equal.

On a Sunday afternoon, quickly following the formation of the association, a new and strange meeting was convened inside the old prison walls. There were present the sheriffs, the ordinary, the governor, the ladies and the women. Doubtless they looked at each other with a mixture of wonder, incredulity, and surprise. The gloomy precincts of Newgate had never witnessed such a spectacle before; the Samaritans of the great city no longer "passed by on the other side," but, at last, had come to grapple with its vice and degradation.

Mrs. Fry read out several rules by which she desired the women to abide; explaining to them the necessity for their adherence to these rules, and the extent to which she invited coöperation and assistance in their enforcement. Unanimously and willingly the prisoners engaged to be bound by them, as well as to assist each other in obedience. It will interest the reader to know what these rules were. They were:—

1. That a woman be appointed for the general supervision of the women.

2. That the women be engaged in needle-work, knitting, or any other suitable employment.

3. That there be no begging, swearing, gaming, card-playing, quarrelling, or universal conversation. That all novels, plays, and other

improper books be excluded ; that all bad words be avoided, and any default in these particulars be reported to the matron.

4. That there be a good yard-keeper, chosen from among the women, to inform them when their friends come ; to see that they leave their work with a monitor when they go to the grat-ing, and that they do not spend any time there except with their friends. If any woman be found disobedient in these respects, the yard-keeper is to report the case to the matron.

5. That the women be divided into classes of not more than twelve, and that a monitor be appointed to each class.

6. That the monitors be chosen from among the most orderly of the women that can read, to superintend the work and conduct of the others.

7. That the monitors not only overlook the women in their own classes, but, if they ob-serve any others disobeying the rules, that they inform the monitor of the class to which such persons may belong, who is immediately to report them to the matron, and the deviations be set down on a slate.

8. That any monitor breaking the rules shall be dismissed from her office, and the most suit-able in the class selected to take her place.

9. That the monitors be particularly careful

to see that women come with clean hands and faces to their work, and that they are quiet during their employment.

10. That at the ringing of the bell at nine o'clock in the morning, the women collect in the work-room to hear a portion of Scripture read by one of the visitors, or the matron ; and that the monitors afterwards conduct the classes thence to their respective wards in an orderly manner.

11. That the women be again collected for reading at 6 o'clock in the evening, when the work shall be given in charge to the matron by the monitors.

12. That the matron keep an exact account of the work done by the women, and of their conduct.

As these rules were read out, the women were requested to raise their hands in token of assent. Not a hand but was held up. In just the same manner the names of the monitors were received, and the appointments ratified. After this business had been concluded, one of the visitors read the twenty-first chapter of St. Matthew's Gospel ; and then ensued a period of solemn silence, according to the custom of the Society of Friends. After that the newly-elected monitors, at the heads of their classes, withdrew to their wards.

The work room was an old disused laundry, now granted by the sheriffs, and fitted up for the purpose. Repaired and whitewashed, it proved a capital vantage-ground whereon to give battle to the old giants of Ignorance, Crime and Vice, and ultimately to conquer them.

The next thing was to obtain a sufficiency of work, and at the same time funds to purchase materials. At first, the most imperative necessity existed for clothing. For a long time the most ample help came from Mrs. Fry's own family circle, although many others contributed various sums. Indeed, the Sheriffs of London on one occasion made a grant of £80 towards these objects, showing thus that, although punitive measures were more in their way, they were really glad to uphold the hands of anybody who would deal with the vexed problems which such hordes of criminals presented.

After the criminals themselves were clothed, their work went to provide garments for the convicts at Botany Bay. Some tradesmen to whom Mrs. Fry applied, willingly resigned these branches of their trade, in order to afford the opportunity of turning the women's industry to account. This was a decided step gained, as the Corporation then learnt how to make the prisoners' labors profitable, and at the same time to avert the mischiefs of vicious idleness.

The ladies tried the school for a month quietly, and found it so successful that they determined to lay a representation before the Sheriffs, asking that this newly-formed agency should be taken under the wing of the Corporation. They wisely considered that the efficiency and continuance of this part of their scheme would be better ensured if it were made part and parcel of the City prison system, than by leaving it to the flunctuating support and management of private benevolence.

In reply to this petition and representation, an answer was received appointing a meeting with the ladies at Newgate. The meeting took place, and a session was held according to the usual rules. The visiting officials were struck with surprise at the altered demeanor of the inhabitants of this hitherto styled "hell upon earth," and were ready to grant what Mrs. Fry chose to ask. The whole plan, both school and manufactory, was adopted as part of the prison system; a cell was granted to the ladies for punishment of refractory prisoners, together with power to confine them therein for short intervals; part of the matron's salary was promised out of the City funds, and benedictions and praises were lavished on the ladies. This assistance in the matter of a matron was a decided help, as, prior to her appointment,

some of the ladies spent much of each day in
the wards personally superintending operations.
So determined were they to win success, that
they even remained during meal times, eating a
little refreshment which they brought with
them. After this appointment, one or two
ladies visited the prison for some time, daily,
spending more or less time there in order to
superintend and direct. Some months after this
a system of work was devised for the "untried
side," but for various reasons, the success in
that department of Newgate was not as marked.
It was found that as long as prisoners indulged
any hope of discharge, they were more careless
about learning industrious and orderly habits.

At this meeting with the civic authorities,
Mrs. Fry offered several suggestions calculated
to promote the well-being of the prisoners,
sedately and gently explaining the reasons for
the necessity of each. They ran thus : —

" 1. Newgate in great want of room. Women
to be under the care of women, matron, turnkeys, and inspecting committee.

" 2. As little communication with their
friends as possible ; only at stated times, except
in very particular cases..

" 3. They must depend on their friends for
neither food nor clothing, but have a sufficiency
allowed them of both.

"4. That employment should be a part of their punishment, and be provided for them by Government. The earnings of work to be partly laid by, partly laid out in small extra indulgences, and, if enough, part to go towards their support.

"5. To work and have their meals together, but sleep separate at night, being classed, with monitors at the head of each class.

"Religious instruction. The kind attention we have had paid us.

"Great disadvantages arise from dependence upon the uncertainty and fluctuations of the Sheriff's funds ; neither soap nor clothing being allowed without its aid, and the occasional help of charitable people."

Two extracts from the civic records prove how warmly the authorities received these suggestions, and in what esteem they held Mrs. Fry and her coadjutors.

SATURDAY, May 3, 1817.

Committee of Aldermen to consider all matters relating to the jails of this city.

Present — The Right Hon. the Lord Mayor, the Sheriffs, and several Aldermen.

The Committee met agreeably to the resolutions of the 29th ult. at the Keeper's House, Newgate, and proceeded from thence, attended by the Sheriffs, to take a view of the jail at Newgate.

The Committee, on viewing that part of it appropriated

to the female prisoners, were attended by Mrs. Elizabeth
Fry and several other ladies, who explained to the Committee the steps they had adopted to induce the female
prisoners to work and to behave themselves in a becoming and orderly manner ; and several specimens of their
work being inspected, the Committee were highly gratified.

At another place is the following entry
After giving date of meeting, and names of
committee present, the minute goes on to say :—

The Committee met at the Mansion House and were
attended by Mrs. Elizabeth Fry and two other ladies, who
were heard in respect of their suggestions for the better
government of the female prisoners in Newgate.

Resolved unanimously : "That the thanks of this Committee be given to Mrs. Fry and the other ladies who have
so kindly exerted themselves with a view to bettering the
condition of the women confined in the jail in Newgate,
and that they be requested to continue their exertions,
which have hitherto been attended with good effect."

Mrs. Fry's journals contain very few particulars relating to her work at this precise time.
It seemed most agreeable to her to work quietly
and unknown as far as the outside public was
concerned. But a lady-worker who was in the
Association has left on record a manuscript
journal from which some extracts may fitly be
given here, as they cast valuable light on both
the work and workers.

We proceeded to the felons' door, the steps of which
were covered with their friends, who were waiting for

admission, laden with the various provisions and other
articles which they required, either as gifts, or to be purchased, as the prisoners might be able to afford. We
entered with this crowd of persons into an ante-room,
the walls of which were covered with the chains and
fetters suspended in readiness for the criminals. A block
and hammer were placed in the centre of it, on which
chains were riveted. The room was guarded with blun-
derbusses mounted on movable carriages. I trembled,
and was sick, and my heart sunk within me, when a
prisoner was brought forward to have his chain lightened,
because he had an inflammation in the ankle. I spoke to
him, for he looked dejected and by no means ferocious.
The turnkey soon opened the first gate of entrance,
through which we were permitted to pass without being
searched, in consequence of orders issued by the sheriffs.
The crowd waited till the men had been searched by the
turnkeys, and the women by a woman stationed for that
purpose in the little room by the door of the entrance.
These searchers are allowed, if they suspect spirits, or
ropes, or instruments of escape to be concealed about
the person, to strip them to ascertain the fact. A melancholy detection took place a few days ago. A poor
woman had a rope found upon her, concealed for the
purpose of liberating her husband, who was then sentenced to death for highway robbery, which sentence was
to be put into execution in a few days. She was, of
course, taken before a magistrate, and ordered into Newgate to await her trial. She was a young and pretty little
Irish woman, with an infant in her arms. After passing
the first floor into a passage, we arrived at the place
where the prisoners' friends communicate with them. It
may justly be termed a sort of iron cage. A considerable
space remains between the grating, too wide to admit of
their shaking hands. They pass into this from the air-

ing-yard, which occupies the centre of the quadrangle round which the building runs, and into which no persons but the visiting ladies, or the persons they introduce, attended by a turnkey, are allowed to enter. A little lodge, in which an under turnkey sleeps, is also considered necessary to render the entrance secure. This yard was clean, and up and down it paraded an emaciated woman, who gave notice to the women of the arrival of their friends. Most of the prisoners were collected in a room newly appropriated for the purpose of hearing a portion of the Sacred Scriptures read to them, either by the matron or by one of the ladies' committee — which last is far preferable. They assemble when the bell rings, as near nine o'clock as possible, following their monitors or wardswomen to the forms which are placed in order to receive them. I think I can never forget the impression made upon my feelings at this sight. Women from every part of Great Britain, of every age and condition below the lower middle rank, were assembled in mute silence, except when the interrupted breathing of their sucking infants informed us of the unhealthy state of these innocent partakers in their parents' punishments. The matron read; I could not refrain from tears. The women wept also; several were under the sentence of death. Swain, who had just received her respite, sat next me; and on my left hand sat Lawrence, *alias* Woodman, surrounded by her four children, and only waiting the birth of another, which she hourly expects, to pay the forfeit of her life, as her husband has done for the same crime a short time before.

Such various, such acute, and such new feelings passed through my mind that I could hardly support the reflection that what I saw was only to be compared to an atom in the abyss of vice, and consequently misery, of this vast metropolis. The hope of doing the least lasting good seemed to vanish, and to leave me in fearful apathy. The prisoners left the room in order. Each monitor took charge of the work in her class on retiring. We proceeded to other wards, some containing forgers, coiners, and thieves; and almost all these vices were engrafted on the most deplorable root of sinful dissipation. Many of the women are married; their families are in some instances permitted to be with them, if very young; their husbands, the partners of their crimes, are often found to be on the men's side of the prison, or on their way to Botany Bay. . . .

They appear to be aware of the true value of character, to know what is right, and to forsake it in action. Finding these feelings yet alive, if properly purified and directed it may become a foundation on which a degree of reformation can be built. Thus they conduct themselves more calmly and decently to each other, they are more orderly and quiet, refrain from bad language, chew tobacco more cautiously, surrender the use of the fireplace, permit doors and windows to be opened and shut to air or warm the prison, reprove their children with less violence, borrow and lend useful articles to each other kindly, put on their attire with modesty, and abstain from slanderous and reproachful words.

None among them was so shocking as an old woman, a clipper of the coin of the realm, whose daughter was by her side, with her infant in her arms, which infant had been born in Bridewell; the grandfather was already transported with several branches of his family, as being coiners. The old woman's face was full of depravity. We next crossed the airing-yard, where many persons were industriously engaged at slop-work, for which they are paid, and after receiving what they require, the rest is kept for them by the Committee, who have a receipt-book, where their earning and their expenditure

may be seen at any time, by the day or week. On entering the untried wards we found the women very different
from those we had just left. They were quarrelling and
very disorderly, neither knowing their future fate, nor
anything like subordination among one another. It
resembles the state of the women on the tried side before
the formation of the Visitors' Association. Not a hand
was employed, except in mischief. One bold creature
was ushered in for committing highway robbery. Many
convicts were arriving, just remanded from the Sessions
House, and their dark associates received them with
applause — such is the unhallowed friendship of sin. We
left this revolting scene and proceeded to the school-room,
situated on the untried side of the prison for want of
room on the tried. The quiet decency of this apartment
was quite a relief, for about twenty young women arose
on our entrance, and stood with their eyes cast on the
ground.

Another extract from the diary of this lady
will be found to describe, in graphic terms, the
visit to the prison recorded in the Corporation
minutes. As one reads the simple and truth-like
story, the scene rises before the mind's eye : —
the party of gentlemen upon their semi-official
visit ; the awe-stricken prisoners, scarcely com-
prehending whether this visit boded ill or well
to them ; and the little company of quiet, godly,
unfashionable Quaker ladies, who were thus
"laying hands" upon the lost of their sex, in
order to reclaim them. Such a picture might
well be transferred to canvas.

Rose early and visited Newgate, where most of the Committee met to receive the Lord Mayor, the Sheriffs, several Aldermen, and some of the Jail Committee. Even the irritable state of city politics does not interfere with this attempt at improvement. The women were assembled as usual, looking particularly clean, and Elizabeth Fry had commenced reading a Psalm, when the whole of this party entered this already crowded room. Her reading was thus interrupted for a short time. She looked calmly on the approaching gentlemen, who, soon perceiving the solemnity of her occupation, stood still midst the multitude, whilst Elizabeth Fry resumed her office and the women their quietude. In an impressive tone she told them she never permitted any trifling circumstance to interrupt the very solemn and important engagement of reading the Holy Scriptures; but in this instance it appeared unavoidable from the unexpected entrance of so many persons, besides which, when opportunity offers, we should pay respect to those in authority over us, to those who administer justice. She thus, with a Christian prudence peculiar to herself, controlled the whole assembly, and subdued the feelings of the prisoners, many of whom were but two well acquainted with the faces of the magistrates, who were themselves touched and astonished at being thus introduced to a state of decorum so new within these walls, and could not help acknowledging how admirably this mode of treatment was adapted to overcome the evil spirit which had so long triumphed there. The usual silence ensued after the reading, then the women withdrew. We could not help feeling particularly glad that the gentlemen were present at the reading. The prisoners crowded around the Lord Mayor and Sheriffs to beg little favors. We had a long conference with these gentlemen relative to this prison and its object, and to the wisest regulations for prison discipline, and the causes of

crime. Indeed, we could not have received more kind
and devoted attention to what was suggested. Elizabeth
Fry's manner seemed to awaken new trains of reflection,
and to place the individual value of these poor creatures
before them in a fresh point of view. The Sheriffs came
to our committee-room. They ordered a cell to be given
up to the Committee for the temporary confinement of
delinquents; it was to be made to appear as formidable
as possible, and we hope never to require it.

The soldiers who guarded Newgate were, at our own
request, dismissed. They overlooked the women's wards,
and rendered them very disorderly. . . . I found poor
Woodman lying-in in the common ward, where she had been
suddenly taken ill; herself and little girl were each doing
very well. She was awaiting her execution at the end of
the month. What can be said of such sights as these?
. . . . I read to Woodman, who is not in the state of mind
we could wish for her; indeed, so unnatural is her situation that one can hardly tell how, or in what manner, to
meet her case. She seems afraid to love her baby, and
the very health which is being restored to her produces
irritation of mind.

This last entry furnishes, incidentally, proof
of the barbarity of the laws of Christian England at that time. Human life was of no account
compared with the robbery of a few shillings, or
the cutting down of a tree. This matter of capital punishment, in its turn, attracted the attention of the Quaker community, together with
other philanthropic individuals, and the statute
book was in time freed from many of the sanguinary enactments which had, prior to that
period, disgraced it.

By this time notoriety began to attend Mrs. Fry's labors, and she was complimented and stared at according to the world's most approved fashion. The newspapers noticed her work; the people at Court talked about it; and London citizens began to realize that in this quiet Quakeress there dwelt a power for good. Given an unusual method of doing good, noticed by the high in place and power, together with praise or criticism by the papers, and, like Lord Byron, the worker wakes some morning to find himself or herself famous. But growing fame did not agree with Elizabeth Fry's moral or spiritual nature. She possessed far too noble a soul to be pleased with it; her responsibility and her success, except so far as they affected the waifs she desired to bless, were matters for her own conscience, and her God. She mentioned in her journal her fears whether or not this public- ity, and the evident respect paid her by the people in power in the city, might not develop worldly pride of self-exaltation in her. Highly- toned and pure as her spirit was, it shrank from any strain of self-seeking or pride. Only such a spirit could have conceived such a work of usefulness ; only such an one could endure the inevitable repulsion which attends such work among the degraded, and conquer.

CHAPTER VII.

EVIDENCE BEFORE THE HOUSE OF COMMONS.

Public attention was so far aroused on the subject of prison discipline, and the condition of
criminals, that a Committee of the House of
Commons was appointed to examine into evidence respecting the prisons of the metropolis.
On the 27th of February, 1818, Mrs. Fry was
examined by this Committee, relative to her
personal experiences of this work, and her own
labors in connection with it. The clear, calm
statements made by her before this Committee
cast considerable light upon her doings, and the
principles upon which she acted. There is no
exaggeration, no braggadocio, no flourish of
philanthropy, — simply a straightforward story
of quiet but persistent endeavors to lessen the
human misery within the walls of the prison at
Newgate; for, hitherto, her efforts had been
confined to that jail.

"*Query.* You applied to the Committee of
the Court of Aldermen?"

"*Ans.* Not at first; I thought it better to

try the experiment for a month, and then to
ask them whether they would second us, and
adopt our measures as their own ; we, therefore,
assembled our women, read over our rules,
brought them work, knitting, and other things,
and our institution commenced; it has now
been about ten months. Our rules have certainly been occasionally broken, but very seldom ; order has generally been observed. I
think I may say we have full power among
them, for one of them said it was more terrible
to be brought up before me than before the
judge, though we use nothing but kindness.
I have never punished a woman during the
whole time, or even proposed a punishment to
them ; and yet I think it is impossible in a well-
ordered house to have rules more strictly
attended to than they are, as far as I order
them, or our friends in general. With regard
to our work, they have made nearly twenty
thousand articles of wearing apparel, the gen-
erality of which is supplied by the slop-shops,
which pay very little. Excepting three out of
this number that were missing, which we really
do not think owing to the women, we have
never lost a single article. They knit from
about sixty to a hundred pairs of stockings and
socks every month ; they spin a little. The
earnings of work, we think, average about eigh-

teenpence per week for each person. This is generally spent in assisting them to live, and helps to clothe them. For this purpose they subscribe out of their small earnings of work about four pounds a month, and we subscribe about eight, which keeps them covered and decent. Another very important point is the excellent effects we have found to result from religious education ; our habit is constantly to read the Scriptures to them twice a day. Many of them are taught, and some of them have been enabled to read a little themselves ; it has had an astonishing effect. I never saw the Scriptures received in the same way, and to many of them they have been entirely new, both the great system of religion and morality contained in them ; and it has been very satisfactory to observe the effect upon their minds. When I have sometimes gone and said it was my intention to read, they would flock up-stairs after me, as if it were a great pleasure I had to afford them."

"You have confined yourself to reading the Scriptures, and pointing out generally the moral lessons that might be derived from them ?"

"Yes, generally so."

"Without inculcating any particular doc-trine ? "

"Nothing but the general Scripture doctrine ;

in short, they are not capable of receiving any other."

"Nothing but the morals of the Scripture,— the duties towards God and man ? "

"That is all ; we are very particular in endeavoring to keep close to that. We consider, from the situation we fill, as it respects the public, as well as the poor creatures themselves, that it would be highly indecorous to press any particular doctrine of any kind, anything beyond the fundamental doctrines of Scripture. We have had considerable satisfaction in observing, not only the improved state of the women in the prison, but we understand from the governor and clergyman at the penitentiary, that those who have been under our care are very different from those who come from other prisons. We also may state that when they left Newgate to go to Botany Bay, such a thing was never known in the prison before as the quietness and order with which they left it ; instead of tearing down everything, and burning it, it was impossible to leave it more peaceably. And as a proof that their moral and religious instruction have had some effect upon their minds, when those poor creatures were going to Botany Bay, the little fund we allowed them to collect for themselves, in a small box under our care, they entreated might all be given to those that were going, those who remained saying that they wished to give up their little share of the profit to the others."

"Do you know anything of the room and accommodation for the women in 1815?"

"I do not; I did not visit it in that year."

"What was it in 1817?"

"Not nearly room enough. If we had room enough to class them, I think a very great deal more might be accomplished. We labor very much in the day, and we see the fruit of our labor: but if we could separate them in the night, I do think that we could not calculate upon the effect which would be produced."

"At present, those convicted for all offenses pass the day together?"

"Very much so; very much intermixed, old and young, hardened offenders with those who have committed only a minor crime, or the first crime; the very lowest of women with respectable married women and maid-servants. It is more injurious than can be described, in its effects and in its consequences. One little instance to prove how beneficial it is to take care of the prisoners, is afforded by the case of a poor woman, for whom we have obtained pardon (Lord Sidmouth having been very kind to us whenever we have applied for the mitigation of punishment since our committee has been formed). We taught her to knit in the prison; she is now living respectably out of it, and in part gains her livelihood by knitting. We generally endeavor to provide for them in degree when they go out. One poor woman to whom we lent money, comes every week to my house, and pays two shillings, as honestly and as punctually as we could desire. We give part, and lend part, to accustom them to habits of punctuality and honesty."

"Is that woman still in Newgate, whose husband was executed, and she herself condemned to death, having eight children?"

"She is."

"Has not her character been very materially changed since she has been under your care?"

"I heard her state to a gentleman going through the other day, that it had been a very great blessing to her at Newgate, and I think there has been a very great change in her. Her case is now before Lord Sidmouth, but we could hardly ask for her immediate liberation."

"What reward, or hope of reward, do you hold out?"

"Rewards form one part of our plan. They not only have the earning of their work, but we endeavor to stimulate them by a system of marks. We divide our women into classes, with a monitor over every class, and our matron at the head. It is the duty of every monitor to take up to the matron every night an account of the conduct of her class, which is set down ; and if they have a certain number of what we call good marks at the end of any fixed period, they have for rewards such prizes as we think proper to give them — generally small articles of cloth-ing, or Bibles and Testaments."

"Be so good as to state, as nearly as you can, what proportion of the women, without your assistance, would be in a state of extreme want ? "

"It is difficult to say ; but I think we average the number of eighty tried women. Perhaps out of that number twenty may live very well, twenty very badly, and the others are supported by their friends in some degree. When I say twenty who live very well, I mention, perhaps, too large a number — perhaps not above ten. I think their receiving support from out-of-doors is most injurious, as it respects their moral prin-ciples, and everything else, as it respects the welfare of the city. There are some very poor people who will almost starve at home, and be induced to do that which is wrong, in order to keep their poor relations who are in prison. It is an unfair tax on such people ; in addition to which, it keeps up an evil communication, and, what is more, I believe they often really encourage the crime by it for which they are put into prison; for these very people, and especially the coiners and passers of bank-notes, are supported by their associates in crime, so that it really tends to keep up their bad practices."

"Do you know whether there is any clothing allowed by the city?"

"Not any. Whenever we have applied or mentioned anything about clothing, we have always found that there was no other resource but our own, excepting that the sheriffs used to clothe the prisoners occasionally. Lately, nobody has clothed them but ourselves; except that the late sheriffs sent us the other day a present of a few things to make up for them."

"There is no regular clothing allowed?"

"It appears to me that there is none of any kind."

"Have you never had prisoners there who have suffered materially for want of clothing?"

"I could describe such scenes as I should hardly think it delicate to mention. We had a woman the other day, on the point of lying-in, brought to bed not many hours after she came in. She had hardly a covering; no stockings, and only a thin gown. Whilst we are there, we can never see a woman in that state without immediately applying to our fund."

"When they come in they come naked, almost?"

"Yes, this woman came in, and we had to send her up almost every article of clothing, and to clothe her baby. She could not be tried the next sessions, but after she had been tried, and when she was discharged, she went out comfortably clothed; and there are many such instances."

"Has it not happened that when gentlemen have come in to see the prison, you have been obliged to stand before the women who were in the prison in a condition not fit to be seen?"

"Yes, I remember one instance in which I was obliged to stand before one of the women to prevent her being seen. We sent down to the matron immediately to get her clothes."

"How long had the woman been in jail?"

"Not long; for we do not, since we have been there, suffer them to be a day without being clothed?"

"What is the average space allowed to each woman to lie upon, taking the average number in the prison?"

"I cannot be accurate, not having measured; from eighteen inches to two feet, I should think."

"By six feet?"

"Yes. I believe the moral discipline of a prison can never be complete while they are allowed to sleep together in one room. If I may be allowed to state it, I should prefer a prison where women were allowed to work together in companies, under proper superintendence ; to have their meals together, and their recreation also ; but I would always have them separated in the night. I believe it would conduce to the health both of body and mind. Their being in companies during the day, tends, under proper regulations, to the advancement of principle and industry, for it affords a stimulus. I should think solitary confinement proper only in atrocious cases. I would divide every woman for a few weeks, until I knew what they were, but I would afterwards regulate them as I have before mentioned."

"Has gaming entirely ceased ? "

"It has of late : they have once been found gaming since we had care of the prison, but I called the women up when I found that some of them had been playing at cards, and represented to them how much I objected to it, and how evil I thought its consequence was, especially to them ; at the same time I stated that if there were cards in the prison, I should consider it a proof of their regard if they would have the candor and the kindness to bring me their packs. I did not expect they would do it, for they would feel they had betrayed themselves by it ; however, I was sitting with the matron,

and heard a gentle tap at the door, and in came
a trembling woman to tell me she had brought
her pack of cards, that she was not aware how
wrong it was, and hoped I would do what I
liked with them. In a few minutes another
came up, and in this way I had five packs of
cards burnt. I assured them that so far from
its being remembered against them, I should
remember them· in another way. I brought
them a present of clothing for what they had
done, and one of them, in a striking manner,
said she hoped I would excuse her being so forward, but, if she might say it, she felt exceedingly disappointed ; she little thought of having
clothing given her, but she had hoped I would
give her a Bible, that she might read the Scriptures. This had been one of the worst girls,
and she had behaved so very badly upon her
trial that it was almost shameful. She conducted herself afterwards in so amiable a manner, that her conduct was almost without a flaw.
She is now in the Penitentiary, and, I hope, will
become a valuable member of society.”

“ You have stated three things which to your
mind are essential to the reformation of a prison:
first, religious instruction ; secondly, classification ; thirdly, employment. Do you think that
any reformation can be accomplished without
employment ? ”

" I should believe it impossible ; we may instruct as we will, but if we allow them their
time, and they have nothing to do, they must
naturally return to their evil practices."

"How many removals of female prisoners
have you had in the last year, in Newgate ; how
many gone to Botany Bay ? "

" Eighteen women ; and thirty-seven to the
Penitentiary."

" Can you state out of what number of convicts these have been in the course of a year ? "

" I do not think I can ; but, of course, out of
many hundreds."

"In fact, has there been only one regular
removal within the last year ? "

" But one. There is one very important thing
which ought to be stated on the subject of
women taking care of women. It has been said
that there were three things which were requisite in forming a prison that would really tend
to the reformation of the women ; but there is
a fourth, viz : that women should be taken care
of entirely by women, and have no male attendants, unless it be a medical man or any minister
of religion. For I am convinced that much
harm arises from the communication, not only
to the women themselves, but to those who have
the care of them."

" In the present arrangement is it not so with
regard to the women ? "

" It is very nearly so ; but if I had a prison completely such as I should like it, it would be a prison quite apart from the men's prison, and into which neither turnkeys nor anyone else should enter but female attendants and the In-specting Committee of Ladies, except, indeed, such gentlemen as come to look after their wel-fare."

" In what does the turnkey interfere now with the prison ? "

" Very little ; and yet there is a certain inter-course which it is impossible for us to prevent. And it must be where there is a prison for women and men, and there are various officers who are men in the prison ; it is impossible that they should be entirely separate. In the pres-ent state of Newgate such a plan as I have in my mind respecting the proper management of women prisoners cannot be put into execution. We must have turnkeys and a governor to refer to ; but I should like to have a prison which had nothing to do with men, except those who attended them spiritually or medically."

" Do you believe men to be as much excluded from all communication with the women now as is possible in the present state of Newgate ? "

" Yes, I think very nearly so. My idea with regard to the employment of women is, that it should be a regular thing undertaken by Government, considering (though, perhaps, I am not the person to speak of that) that there are so many to provide for ; there is the army and navy, and so many things to provide for them ; why should not the Government make use of the prisoners ? But I consider it of the utmost importance, and quite indispensable for the conduct of these institutions, that the prisoners should have part of the earnings of their work for their own use ; a part they might be allowed to take for tea, sugar, etc., but a part should be laid by that there may be some provision for them when they leave the prison, without their returning to their immoral practices. This is the case, I believe, in all prisons well regulated, both on the continent of Europe and America. In a prison under proper regulation, where they had very little communication with their friends, where they were sufficiently well fed and clothed, constantly employed and instructed, and taken care of by women, I have not the least doubt that wonders would be performed, and that many of those, now the most profligate and worst of characters, would turn out valuable members of society. After having said what I have respecting the care of women, I will just add that I believe that if there were a prison fitted up for us, which we might visit as inspectors, if employment were found for our women, little or no communication with the city, and room given to class them, with female servants only, if there were a thousand of the most unruly women they would be in excellent order in one week ; of that I have not the least doubt."

The natural consequence of this evidence was increased publicity and increased usefulness ; the first to Mrs. Fry's sorrow, and the second to her great joy. Much as she desired to work in secret, it was not possible; nor, all things considered, was it for the best that she should do so. The prison reform which she desired to see carried out was destined to cover, and indeed, required a larger area than she could obtain. But the fame of her improvements at Newgate, the tales of lions being turned into lambs, and sinners into saints, by the exertions of this woman and her band of helpers, caught the ear and thrilled the heart of the public. The excitement produced among the community deepened and intensified as more of the work became revealed. Representatives of every class in society visited the gloomy precincts of Newgate, in order to see and hear for themselves how far these wonders extended, while at every hospital and fashionable board the theme was ever the same. At one time Mrs. Fry was at Newgate in company with the Chancellor of the Exchequer and other celebri-

ties ; while at another time she appeared at the
Mansion House, honored by royalty, the " observed of all observers." The Queen of England, among others, was anxious to see and
converse with the woman who had with such
quiet power succeeded in solving a great social
problem, and that where municipal authorities
had failed.

Mrs. Fry, although belonging to that religious community which takes not off the hat to
royalty, possessed loyal feelings.   Therefore,
when Queen Charlotte commanded her to
appear at the Mansion House, in order to be
formerly presented to her, with true womanly
grace and respect she hastened to obey. It was
intended that the presentation should have
taken place in the drawing-room, but by some
mistake Mrs. Fry was conducted to the Egyptian Hall, where a number of school-children
were waiting to be examined.   Mrs. Fry occupied a post near the platform ; and after a little
time the Queen, now aged and infirm, perceived
her. As soon as the examination of the children was over she advanced to Mrs. Fry.   Her
Majesty's small figure, her dress blazing with
diamonds, her courtesy and kindness as she
spoke to the now celebrated Quakeress, who
stood outwardly calm in the costume of her
creed, and just a little flushed with the un-

wonted excitement, attracted universal homage.
Around stood several bishops, peers, and peer-
esses ; the hall was filled with spectators, while
outside the crowd surged and swayed as crowds
are wont to do. For a few moments the two
women spoke together; then the strict rules of
etiquette were overcome by the enthusiasm of
the assembly and a murmur of applause, followed by a ringing English cheer, went up.
This cheer was repeated by the crowd outside,
again and again, while the most worldly butter-
fly that ever buzzed and fluttered about a court
learnt that day that there was in goodness and
benevolence something better than fashion and
nobler than rank. This was almost, if not
quite, Queen Charlotte's last public appearance;
she very soon afterwards passed to her rest,
"old and full of days.'

Ever true to her own womanly instincts, we
find Mrs. Fry lamenting, in her journal, that
herself and the prison are becoming quite a
show ; yet, on the other hand, she recognized
the good of this inconvenience, inasmuch as
the work spread among all classes of society.
Various opinions were passed upon her, and on
one occasion a serious misunderstanding with
Lord Sidmouth, respecting a case of capital
punishment, severely tried her constancy. Some
carping critics found fault, others were envious,

others censorious and shallow ; but neither good report nor evil report moved her very greatly, although possibly at times they were the subject of much inward struggle.

This question of Prison Reform at last reached Parliament. In June, 1818, the Marquis of Lansdowne moved an address to the Prince Regent, asking an inquiry into the state of the prisons of the United Kingdom. He made a remarkable speech, quoting facts relating to the miseries of the jails, and concluded with a high eulogium on Mrs. Fry's labors among the criminals of Newgate, giving her the title "Genius of Good." This step drew public attention still more to the matter and prison-visiting and prison reform became the order of the day. As public attention had been aroused, and public sympathy had been gained for the cause, it is not wonderful that beneficial legislative measures were at last carried.

Meanwhile the ladies continued their good work. It was one of the cardinal points of their creed, that it was not good for the criminals to have much intercourse with their friends outside. In past times unlimited beer had been carried into Newgate ; at least the quantity so disposed of was only limited by the amount of ready cash or credit at the disposal of the criminals and their friends. This had been stopped with the happiest results, and now it seemed time to adopt some measures which should secure some little additional comfort for the prisoners. In order to effect this a sub-matron, or gate-keeper, was engaged, who assisted in the duties at the lodge, and kept a small shop "between gates," where tea, sugar, and other little comforts could be purchased by the prisoners out of their prison earnings. This step was a successful one, for with the decrease of temptation from without, came an increase of comfort from within, provided they earned money and obeyed rules. Plenty of work could be done, seeing that they all required more or less clothing, while Botany Bay could take any number of garments to be utilized for the members of the penal settlement there.

Two months after Lord Lansdowne's motion was made in Parliament, Mrs. Fry, together with Joseph John Gurney, his wife, and her own daughter, Rachel, went into Scotland on a religious and philanthropic tour. The chief object of this journey seems to have been the visitation of Friends' Meetings in that part of the kingdom ; but the prison enterprise was by no means forgotten. In her journal she records visits to meetings of Friends held at Aberdeen, Edinburgh, Glasgow, Liverpool and Knowsley.

At the latter place they were guests of the Earl
of Derby, and much enjoyed the palatial
hospitality which greeted them. They made a
point of visiting most of the jails and bride-
wells in the towns through which they passed,
finding in some of them horrors far surpassing
anything that Newgate could have shown them
even in its unreformed days. At Haddington
four cells, allotted to prisoners of the tramp
and criminal class, were "very dark, excessively
dirty, had clay floors, no fire-places, straw in one
corner for a bed, and in each of them a tub, the
receptacle for all filth." Iron bars were used
upon the prisoners so as to become instruments
of torture. In one cell was a poor young man
who was a lunatic — whence nobody knew. He
had been subject to the misery and torture of
Haddington jail for eighteen months, without
once leaving his cell for an airing. No clothes
were allowed, no medical man attended those
who were incarcerated, and a chaplain never
entered there, while the prison itself was destitute of any airing-yard. The poor debtors,
whether they were few or many, were all confined in one small cell not nine feet square,
where one little bed served for all.

At Kinghorn, Fifeshire, a young laird had
languished in a state of madness for six years
in the prison there, and had at last committed

suicide. Poor deranged human nature flew to death as a remedy against torture. At Forfar, prisoners were chained to the bedstead; at Berwick, to the walls of their cells; and at Newcastle to a ring in the floor. The two most objectionable features in Scotch prisons, as appears from Mr. Gurney's "Notes" of this tour, were the treatment of debtors, and the cruelties used to lunatics. Both these classes of individuals were confined as criminals, and treated with the utmost cruelty.

According to Scotch law, the jailer and magistrates who committed the debtor became responsible for the debt, supposing the prisoner to have effected his escape. Self-interest, therefore, prompted the adoption of cruel measures to ensure the detention of the unfortunate debtor; while helpless lunatics were wholly at the mercy of brutalized keepers who were responsible to hardly any tribunal. Of the horrors of that dark, terrible time within those prison-walls, few records appear; few cared to probe the evil, or to propose a remedy. The archives of Eternity alone contain the captive's cries, and the lamentations of tortured lunatics. Only one Eye penetrated the dungeons; one Ear heard. Was not Elizabeth Fry and her coadjutors doing a god-like work? And when she raised the clarion cry that *Reforma-tion*, not *Revenge*, was the object of punishment, she shook these old castles of Giant Despair to their foundations.

CHAPTER VIII.

THE GALLOWS AND ENGLISH LAWS.

About this period the subject of Capital Punishment largely attracted Mrs. Fry's attention. The attitude of Quakers generally towards the punishment of death, except for murder in the highest degree, was hostile ; but Mrs. Fry's constant intercourse with inmates in the condemned cell fixed her attention in a very painful manner upon the subject. For venial crimes, men and women, clinging fondly to life, were swung off into eternity ; and neither the white lips of the philanthropist, nor the official ones of the appointed chaplain, could comfort the dying. Among these dying ones were many women, who were executed for simply passing forged Bank of England notes ; but as the bank had plenary powers to arrange to screen certain persons who were not to die, these were allowed to get off with a lighter punishment by pleading "Guilty to the minor count." The condemned cell was never, however, without its occupant, nor the gallows destitute of its prey. So Dra-

conian were the laws of humane and Christain
England, at this date, that had they been strictly
carried out, at least four executions daily, exclu-
sive of Sundays, would have taken place in this
realm.

According to Hepworth Dixon, and contemporary authorities, the sanguinary measures of
the English Government for the punishment of
crimes dated from about the time of the Jacob-
ite rebellion, in 1745. Prior to that time, adven-
turers of every grade, the idle, vicious, and
unemployed, had found an outlet for their turbu-
lence and their energies in warfare — engaging
on behalf of the Jacobites, or the Government,
according as it suited their fancy. But when
the House of Hanover conquered, and the trade
of war became spoiled within the limits of
Great Britain, troops of these discharged soldiers took to a marauding life ; the high roads
became infested with robbers, and crimes of
violence were frequent. Alarmed at the license
displayed by these Ishmaelites, the Government
of the day arrayed its might against them, enact-
ing such sanguinary measures that at first sight
it seemed as if the deliberate intent were to literally cut them off and root them out from the
land. That era was indeed a bloodthirsty one
in English jurisprudence.

Enactments were passed in the reign of the

second George, whereby it was made a capital crime to rob the mail, or any post-office ; to kill, steal, or drive away any sheep or cattle, with intention to steal, or to be accessory to the crime. The "Black Act," first passed in the reign of George I., and enlarged by George II., punished by hanging, the hunting, killing, stealing, or wounding any deer in any park or forest; maiming or killing any cattle, destroying any fish or fish-pond, cutting down or killing any tree planted in any garden or orchard, or cutting any hop-bands in hop plantations. Forgery, smuggling, coining, passing bad coin, or forged notes, and shop-lifting ; all were punishable by death. From a table published by Janssen, and quoted from Hepworth Dixon, we find that in twenty-three years, from 1749 to 1771, eleven hundred and twenty-one persons were condemned to death in London alone. The offenses for which these poor wretches received sentence included those named above, in addition to seventy-two cases of murder, two cases of riot, one of sacrilege, thirty-one of returning from transportation, and four of enlisting for foreign service. Of the total number condemned, six hundred and seventy-eight were actually hanged, while the remainder either died in prison, were transported, or pardoned. As four hundred and one persons were transported, a very small number indeed

obtained deliverance either by death or pardon.
In fact, scarcely any extenuating circumstances
were allowed; so that in some cases cruelty
seemed actually to have banished justice. It is
recorded, as one of these cases, that a young
woman with a babe at the breast, was hanged
for stealing from a shop a piece of cloth of the
value of five shillings. The poor woman was
the destitute wife of a young man whom the
press-gang had captured and carried off to sea,
leaving her and her babe to the mercy of the
world. Utterly homeless and starving, she stole
to buy food; but a grateful country requited
the services of the sailor-husband by hanging
the wife.

The *certainty* of punishment became nullified
by the *severity* of the laws. Humane individuals
hesitated to prosecute, especially for forgery;
while juries seized upon every pretext to return
verdicts of "Not guilty." Reprieves were frequent, for the lives of many were supplicated,
and successfully; so that the death-penalty was
commuted into transportation. Caricaturists,
writers, philanthropists, divines—all united in
the chorus of condemnation against the bloody
enactments which secured such a crop for the
gallows. Men, women, girls, lads and idiots,
all served as food for it. Jack Ketch had a merry
time of it, while society looked on well pleased,

for the most part. Those appointed to sit in the seat of justice sometimes defended this state of things. One of the worthies of the "good old times" — Judge Heath — notorious because of his partiality for hanging, is reported to have said : "If you imprison at home, the criminal is soon thrown back upon you hardened in guilt. If you transport you corrupt infant societies, and sow the seeds of atrocious crimes over the habitable globe. There is no regenerating a felon in this life. And, for his own sake, as well as for the sake of society, I think it better to hang."

As a caricaturist George Cruikshank entered the field, and waged battle on behalf of the poor wretches who swung at the gallows for passing forged Bank of England notes. He drew a note resembling the genuine one, and entitled it "Bank note, *not* to be imitated." A copy of this caricature now lies before us. It bears on its face a representation of a large gallows, from which eleven criminals, three of whom are women, are dangling, dead. In the upper left hand corner, Britannia is represented as surrounded by starving, wailing creatures, and surmounted by a hideous death's head. Underneath is a rope coiled around the portraits of twelve felons who have suffered ; while, running down, to form a border, are fetters arranged in zig-zag fashion. Across the note run these words, "*Ad lib., ad lib.,* I promise to perform during the issue of Bank notes easily imitated, and until the resumption of cash payments, or the abolition of the punishment of death, for the Governors and Company of the Bank of England.—J. KETCH." The note is a unique production, and must have created an enormous sensation. Cruikshank's own story, writing in 1876, is this :—

Fifty-eight years back from this date there were one-pound Bank of England notes in circulation, and, unfortunately, many forged notes were in circulation also, or being passed, the punishment for which offense was in some cases transportation, in others DEATH. At this period, having to go early to the Royal Exchange one morning, I passed Newgate jail, and saw several persons suspended from the gibbet; *two* of these were women who had been executed for passing one-pound forged notes.

I determined, if possible, to put a stop to such terrible punishments for such a crime, and made a sketch of the above note, and then an etching of it.

Mr. Hone published it, and it created a sensation. The Directors of the Bank of England were exceedingly wroth. The crowd around Hone's shop in Ludgate Hill was so great that the Lord Mayor had to send the police to clear the street. The notes were in such demand that they could not be printed fast enough, and I had to sit up all one night to etch another plate. Mr. Hone realized above £700, and I had the satisfaction of knowing that no man or woman was ever hanged after this for passing one-pound Bank of England notes.

The issue of my " Bank Note not to be Imitated "
not only put a stop to the issue of any more Bank of
England one-pound notes, but also put a stop to the punishment of death for such an offense — not only for that,
but likewise for forgery — and then the late Sir Robert
Peel revised the penal code; so that the final effect of
my note was to stop hanging for all minor offenses, and
has thus been the means of saving thousands of men
and women from being hanged.

It may be that the great caricaturist claims
almost too much when he says that the publication of his note eventually stopped hanging
for all minor offenses ; but certainly there is no
denying that this publication was an important
factor in the agitation.

It is said that George III. kept a register of
all the cases of capital punishment, that he
entered in it all names of felons sentenced to
death, with dates and particulars of convictions,
together with remarks upon the reasons which
induced him to sign the warrants. It is also
said that he frequently rose from his couch at
night to peruse this fatal list, and that he shut
himself up closely in his private apartments
during the hours appointed for the execution
of criminals condemned to death.

Tyburn ceased to be the place of execution
for London in 1783 ; from that year Newgate
witnessed most of these horrors.

Philanthropists of every class were, at the

period of Mrs. Fry's career now under review, considering this matter of capital punishment, and taking steps to restrain the infliction of the death penalty. The Gurney family among Quakers, William Wilberforce, Sir James Mackintosh, Sir Samuel Romilly, and others, were all working hard to this end. In 1819 William Wilberforce presented a petition from the Society of Friends to Parliament against death punishment for crimes other than murder. Writing at later dates upon this subject, Joseph John Gurney says: "I cannot say that my spirit greatly revolts against life for life, though capital punishment for anything short of this appears to me to be execrable." And, again, "I cannot in conscience take any step towards destroying the life of a fellow-creature whose crime against society affects my property only. I am in possession, like other men, of the feelings of common humanity, and to aid and abet in procuring the destruction of any man living would be to me extremely distressing and horrible." As a banker, Mr. Gurney felt that the punishment for forgery should be heavy and sharp, but less than death. In the Houses of Parliament various efforts were made to obtain the commutation of the death penalty, and when in 1810 the Peers rejected Sir Samuel Romilly's bill to remove the penalty for shop-lifting, the Dukes of Sussex and Gloucester joined some of the Peers in signing a protest against the law. The time appeared to be ripe for agitation ; all classes of society reverenced human life more than of old, and desired to see it held less cheap by the ministers of justice.

According to Mrs. Fry's experience, the punishment of death tended neither to the security of the people, the reformation of any prisoner, nor the diminution of crime. Felons who suffered death for light offenses looked upon themselves as martyrs — martyrs to a cruel law — and believed that they had but to meet death with fortitude to secure a blissful hereafter. This fearful opiate carried many through the terrible ordeal outwardly calm and resigned.

Among the condemned ones was Harriet Skelton, a woman who had been detected passing forged Bank of England notes. She was described as prepossessing, "open, confiding, expressing strong feelings on her countenance, but neither hardened in depravity nor capable of cunning." Her behavior in prison was exceptionally good ; so good, indeed, that some of the depraved inmates of Newgate supposed her to have been condemned to death because of her fitness for death. She had evidently been more sinned against than sinning; the man whom she lived with, and who was ardently loved by her, had used her as his instrument for passing these false notes. Thus she had been lured to destruction.

After the decision had been received from the Lords of the Council, Skelton was taken into the condemned cell to await her doom. To this cell came numerous visitors, attracted by compassion for the poor unfortunate who tenanted it, and each one eager to obtain the commutation of the cruel sentence. It was one thing to read of one or another being sentenced to death, but quite another to behold a woman, strong in possession of, and desire for life, fated to be swung into eternity before many days because of circulating a false note at the behest of a paramour. Mrs. Fry needed not the many persuasions she received to induce her to put forth the most unremitting exertions on behalf of Skelton. She obtained an audience of the Duke of Gloucester, and urged every circumstance which could be urged in extenuation of the crime, entreating for the woman's life. The royal duke remembered the old days at Norwich, when Elizabeth had been known in fashionable society and had figured somewhat as a belle, and he bent a willing ear to her request. He visited Newgate, escorted by Mrs. Fry, and saw for himself the agony in that condemned cell. Then he accompanied her to the bank directors, and applied to Lord Sidmouth personally, but all in vain. It was not blood for blood, nor life for life, but blood for "filthy lucre;" so the poor woman was hung in obedience to the inexorable ferocity of the law and its administrators.

On this occasion Mrs. Fry was seriously distressed in mind. She had vehemently entreated for the poor creature's life, stating that she had had the offer of pleading guilty only to the minor count, but had foolishly rejected it in hope of obtaining a pardon. The question at issue on this occasion was the power of the bank directors to virtually decide as to the doom of the accused ones. Mrs. Fry made assertions and gave instances which Lord Sidmouth assumed to doubt. Further than this, he was seriously annoyed at the noise this question of capital punishment was making in the land, and though not necessarily a cruel or blood-thirsty man, the Home Secretary shrank from meddling too much with the criminal code of England. This misunderstanding was a source of deep pain to the philanthropist, and, accompanied by Lady Harcourt, she endeavored to remove Lord Sidmouth's false impressions, but in vain. While smarting under this wound, received in the interests of humanity, she had to go to the Mansion House by command of

Her Majesty Queen Charlotte, to be presented.
Thus, very strangely, and against her will, she
was thrust forward into the very foremost
places of public observation and repute. She
recorded the matter in her journal, in her own
characteristic way : —

"Yesterday I had a day of ups and downs, as far as
the opinions of man are concerned, in a remarkable
degree. I found that there was a grievous misunderstanding between Lord Sidmouth and myself, and that
some things I had done had tried him exceedingly;
indeed, I see that I have mistaken my conduct in some
particulars respecting the case of poor Skelton, and in
the efforts made to save her life, I too incautiously spoke
of some in power. When under great humiliation in
consequence of this, Lady Harcourt, who most kindly
interested herself in the subject, took me with her to
the Mansion House, rather against my will, to meet
many of the royal family at the examination of some
large schools. Among the rest, the Queen was there.
There was quite a buzz when I went into the Egyptian
Hall, where one or two thousand people were collected;
and when the Queen came to speak to me, which she
did very kindly, I am told that there was a general
clap. I think I may say this hardly raised me at all;
I was so very low from what had occurred before. . . .
My mind has not recovered this affair of Lord Sidmouth, and finding that the bank directors are also
affronted with me added to my trouble, more particularly
as there was an appearance of evil in my conduct; but,
I trust, no greater fault in reality than a want of prudence in that which I expressed."

The Society of Friends had always been opposed to capital punishment. Ten years previously, Sir Samuel Romilly had determined to attack these sanguinary enactments, one by one, in order to ensure success. He began, therefore, with the Act of Queen Elizabeth, "which made it a capital offense to steal privately from the person of another." William Allen records in the same year, 1808, the formation of a "Society for Diffusing Information on the Subject of Punishment by Death." This little band worked with Sir Samuel until his painful death in 1818 ; while Dr. Parr, Jeremy Bentham, and Dugald Stewart aided the enterprise by words of encouragement, both in public and in private. In Joseph John Gurney's Memoirs, it is stated that Dr. Lushington declared his opinion that the poor criminal was thus hurried out of life and into eternity by means of the perpetration of another crime far greater, for the most part, than any which the sufferer had committed.

The feeling grew, and in place of the indifference and scorn of human life which had formerly characterized society, there sprang up an eager desire to save life, except for the crime of murder. In May, 1821, Sir James Mackintosh introduced a bill for "Mitigating the Severity of Punishment in Certain Cases of

Forgery, and Crimes connected therewith."
Buxton, in advocating this measure, says truly:

> The people have made enormous strides in all that
> tends to civilize and soften mankind, while the laws have
> contracted a ferocity which did not belong to them in
> the most savage period of our history ; and, to such ex-
> tremes of distress have they proceeded that I do believe
> there never was a law so harsh as British law, or so
> merciful and humane a people as the British people.
> And yet to this mild and merciful people is left the execu-
> tion of that rigid and cruel law.

This measure was defeated, but the numbers
of votes were so nearly equal, that the defeat
was actually a victory.

Time went on. In 1831, Sir Robert Peel
took up the gauntlet against capital punishment, and endeavored to induce Parliament to
abolish the death-penalty for forgery ; the House
of Commons voted its abolition, but the Lords
restored the clauses retaining the penalty. One
thousand bankers signed a petition praying that
the vote of the Commons might be sustained,
but in vain ; still, in deference to public opinion,
after this the death-penalty was not inflicted
upon a forger. Nevertheless, there remained
plenty of food for the gallows. An incendiary,
as well as a sheep-stealer, was liable to capital
punishment ; and so severely was the law
strained upon these points, that he who set fire

to a rick in a field, as well as he who found a half-dead sheep and carried it home, was condemned without mercy. But the advocates of mercy continued their good work until, finally, the gallows became the penalty for only those offenses which concerned human life and high treason.

CHAPTER IX.

MORE work opened before the indefatigable worker. Frequently batches of female convicts were despatched to New South Wales, and, according to the custom at Newgate, departure was preceded by total disregard of order. Windows, furniture, clothing, all were wantonly destroyed; while the procession from the prison to the convict ship was one of brutal, debasing riot. The convicts were conveyed to Deptford, in open wagons, accompanied by the rabble and scum of the populace. These crowds followed the wagons, shouting to the prisoners, defying all regulations, and inciting them to more defiance of rules. Some of the convicts were laden with irons; others were chained together by twos. Mrs. Fry addressed herself first to the manner of departure, and, rightly judging that the open wagons conduced to much disorder, prevailed on the governor of Newgate to engage hackney-coaches for the occasion. Further, she promised the women that, provided they would behave in an orderly manner, she, together with a few other ladies, would accompany them to the ship. Faithful to her promise, her carriage closed the line of hackney-coaches ; three or four ladies were with her, and thus, in a fashion at once strangely quiet and novel, the transports reached the place of embarkation.

There were one hundred and twenty-eight convicts that day ; no small number upon which to experimentalize. As soon as they reached the ship they were herded together below decks like so many cattle, with nothing to do but to curse, swear, fight, recount past crimes, relate foul stories, or plot future evil. True, there was some attempt at order and classification, for they were divided into messes of six each, and Mrs. Fry eagerly seized upon this arrange-ment to form a basis of control. She proposed to the convicts that they should be arranged in classes of twelve, according to ages and crimi-nality ; to this they assented. A class thus fur-nished two messes, while over each class was placed one of the most steady convicts, in order to enforce the rules as much as possible. She provided in this way for superintendence.

The next arrangement concerned work for the women, and instruction for the children. "Sa-tan finds some mischief still for idle hands to

do ;" accordingly the ladies looked about for
plans and methods whereby the enforced weari-
ness of a long voyage should be counteracted.
They had heard that patch-work and fancy-work
found a ready sale in New South Wales, so they
hit upon a scheme which should ensure success
in more ways than one. Having made known
their dilemma, and their desires, they were
cheered by receiving from some wholesale
houses in London sufficient remnants of cotton
print and materials for knitting to furnish all
the convicts with work. There was ample time
to perfect all arrangements, seeing that the ship
lay at Deptford about five weeks ; as the result of
Mrs. Fry's journeys to and fro, every woman had
given to her the chance of benefiting herself.
In this way they were informed that if they
chose to devote the leisure of the voyage to
making up the materials thus placed in their
hands, they would be allowed upon arrival at
the colony to dispose of the articles for their
own profit.

There was thus a new stimulus to exertion
as well as a collateral good. Hitherto, no refuge,
home, or building of any description had existed
for the housing of the women when landed at
the port of disembarkation. There was "not
so much as a hut in which they could take
refuge, so that they were literally driven to vice,

or left to lie in the streets." The system of convict-management at that date was one of compulsory labor, or mostly so. This plan tended to produce tyranny, insubordination, deception, vice, and " the social evil." In the case of men, Captain Mackonochie testified that they were sullen, lazy, insubordinate and vicious; the women, if not engaged quickly in respectable domestic service, and desirous of being kept respectable, become curses to the colony. But by the means adopted by Mrs. Fry each woman was enabled to earn sufficient money to provide for board and lodging until some opening for a decent maintenance presented itself. They thus obtained a fair start.

Provision was also made for instruction of both women and children on board ship. It may be asked how children came there ? Generally they were of tender years and the offspring of vice; the authorities could do nothing with them ; so, perforce, they were allowed to accompany their mothers. Out of the batch on board this transport-vessel, fourteen were found to be of an age capable of instruction. A small space was, therefore, set apart in the stern of the vessel for a school-room, and there, daily, under the tuition of one of the women better taught than the rest, these waifs of humanity learned to read, knit and sew. This slender stock of learning was better than none, wherewith to commence life at the Antipodes.

Almost daily, for five weeks, Mrs. Fry and her coadjutors visited the vessel, laboring to these good ends. Ultimately, however, the *Maria* had to sail, and many were the doubts and fears as to whether the good work begun would be carried on when away from English shores. No matron was there to superintend and to direct the women : if they continued in the path marked out for them, their poor human nature could not be so fallen after all. Mrs. Fry had a kind of religious service with the convicts the last time she visited them. She occupied a position near the door of the cabin, with the women facing her, and ranged on the quarter-deck, while the sailors occupied different positions in the rigging and on other vantage points. As Mrs. Fry read in a solemn voice some passages from her pocket-Bible, the sailors on board the other ships leaned over to hear the sacred words. After the reading was done, she knelt down, and commended the party of soon-to-be exiles to God's mercy, while those for whom she prayed sobbed bitterly that they should see her face no more. Does it not recall the parting of Paul with the elders at Miletus ? Doubtless the memory of that simple service was in after days often the only link between some of those women and goodness.

As time went on, many anxious remembrances and hopes were cast after the convicts who had been shipped to New South Wales. To her sorrow, she found, from the most reliable testimony, that once the poor lost wretches were landed in the colony, they were placed in circumstances that absolutely nullified all the benevolent work which had gone before, and were literally driven by force of circumstances to their destruction. The female convicts, from the time of their landing, were "without shelter, without resources, and without protection. Rations, or a small amount of provision, sufficient to maintain life, they certainly had allotted to them daily ; but a place to sleep in, or money to obtain shelter or necessary clothing for themselves, and, when mothers, for their children, they were absolutely without." An interesting but sad letter was received by Mrs. Fry from the Rev. Samuel Marsden, chaplain at Paramatta, New South Wales, and although long, it affords so much information on this question, that no apology is required for introducing it here. As the testimony of an eye-witness it is valuable :—

HONORED MADAM,

Having learned from the public papers, as well as from my friends in England, the lively interest you have taken in promoting the temporal and eternal welfare of those unhappy females who fall under the sentence of the law, I am induced to address a few lines to you respecting such as visit our distant shores. It may be gratifying to you, Madam, to hear that I meet with those wretched exiles, who have shared your attentions, and who mention your maternal care with gratitude and affection. From the measures you have adopted, and the lively interest you have excited in the public feeling, on the behalf of these miserable victims of vice and woe, I now hope the period is not very distant when their miseries will be in some degree alleviated. I have been striving for more than twenty years to obtain for them some relief, but hitherto have done them little good. It has not been in my power to move those in authority to pay much attention to their wants and miseries. I have often been urged in my own mind, to make an appeal to the British nation, and to lay their case before the public.

In the year 1807, I returned to Europe. Shortly after my arrival in London, I stated in a memorial to His Grace the Archbishop of Canterbury the miserable situation of the female convicts, to His Majesty's Government at the Colonial Office, and to several members of the House of Commons. From the assurances that were then made, that barracks should be built for the accomodation of the female convicts, I entertained no doubt but that the Government would have given instructions to the Governor to make some provisions for them. On my return to the colony, in 1810, I found things in the same state I left them; five years after my again arriving in the colony, I took the liberty to speak to the Governor, as opportunity afforded, on the subject in question, and was surprised to learn that no instructions had been communicated to His Excellency from His Majesty's Government, after what had passed between me and

those in authority at home, relative to the state of the
female convicts. At length I resolved to make an official
statement of their miserable situation to the Governor,
and, if the Governor did not feel himself authorized to
build a barrack for them, to transmit my memorial to my
friends in England, with His Excellency's answer, as a
ground for them to renew my former application to Government for some relief. Accordingly, I forwarded my
memorial, with a copy of the Governor's answer, home
to more than one of my friends. I have never been convinced that no instructions were given by His Majesty's
Government to provide barracks for the female convicts;
on the contrary, my mind is strongly impressed in that
instructions *were* given; if they were not, I can only say
that this was a great omission, after the promises that
were made. I was not ignorant that the sending home of
my letter to the Governor and his answer, would subject
me to the censure as well as the displeasure of my
superiors. I informed some of my friends in England,
as well as in the colony, that if no attention was paid to
the female convicts, I was determined to lay their case
before the British nation; and then I was certain, from
the moral and religious feeling which pervades all ranks,
that redress would be obtained. However, nothing has
been done yet to remedy the evils of which I complain.
For the last five and twenty years many of the convict
women have been driven to vice to obtain a loaf of bread,
or a bed to lie upon. To this day there never has been
a place to put the female convicts in when they land from
the ships. Many of the women have told me with tears
their distress of mind on this account; some would have
been glad to have returned to the paths of virtue if they
could have found a hut to live in without forming improper connections. Some of these women, when they

have been brought before the magistrate, and I have remonstrated with them for their crime, have replied, "I have no other means of living; I am compelled to give my weekly allowance of provisions for my lodgings, and I must starve or live in vice." I was well aware that this statement was correct, and was often at a loss what to answer. It is not only the calamities that these wretched women and their children suffer that are to be regretted, but the general corruption of morals that such a system establishes in this rising colony, and the ruin their example spreads through all the settlements. The male convicts in the service of the Crown, or in that of individuals, are tempted to rob and plunder continually, to supply the urgent necessities of those women.

All the female convicts have not run the same lengths in vice. All are not equally hardened in crime, and it is most dreadful that all should alike, on their arrival here, be liable and exposed to the same dangerous temptations, without any remedy. I rejoice, Madam, that you reside near the seat of Government, and may have it in your power to call the attention of His Majesty's Ministers to this important subject — a subject in which the entire welfare of these settlements is involved. If proper care be taken of the women, the colony will prosper, and the expenses of the mother-country will be reduced. On the contrary, if the morals of the female convicts are wholly neglected, as they have been hitherto, the colony will be only a nursery for crime. . . .

Your good intentions and benevolent labors will all be abortive if the exiled females, on their arrival in the colony, are plunged into every ruinous temptation and sort of vice — which will ever be the case till some barrack is provided for them. Great evils in a state cannot soon be remedied. . . . I believe the Governor has got instruc-

tions from home to provice accommodation for the female convicts, and I hope in two or three years to see them lodged in a comfortable barrack; so that none shall be lost for want of a hut to lie in. If a communication be kept up on a regular plan between this colony and London, much good may be done for the poor female convicts. It was the custom for some years, when a ship with female convicts arrived, soldiers, convicts, and settlers were allowed to go on board and take their choice; this custom does not now openly obtain countenance and sanction, but when they are landed they have no friend, nor any accommodation, and therefore are glad to live with anyone who can give them protection; so the real moral state of these females is little improved from what it always has been, nor will it be the least improved till they can be provided with a barrack. The neglect of the female convicts in this country is a disgrace to our national character, as well as a national sin. Many do not live out half their days, from their habits of vice. When I am called to visit them on their dying beds, my mind is greatly pained, my mouth is shut; I know not what to say to them. . . . To tell them of their crimes is to upbraid them with misfortune; they will say, " Sir, you know how I was situated. I do not wish to lead the life I have done; I know and lament my sins, but necessity compeiled me to do what my conscience condemned."
. . . Many, again, I meet with who think these things no crime, because they believe their necessities compel them to live in their sins. Hence their consciences are so hardened through the deceitfulness of sin, that death itself gives them little concern. . . .

I have the honor to be, Madam,

Your most obedient humble servant,

SAMUEL MARSDEN.

This appeal was not disregarded : in due time
official apathy and inertness fled before the
national cry for reform. Meanwhile, Mrs. Fry
continued her efforts on behalf of the convicts
on board the transports, ever urging upon those
in power the imperative necessity for placing
the women under the charge of matrons. They
still continued on the old plan, and were wholly
in the power of the sailors, except for such
supervision as the Naval Surgeon Superintendent could afford. Some little improvements
had taken place, since that first trip to the
Maria convict-ship, but very much still remained
to be done. To these floating prisons, frequently detained for weeks in the Thames, Mrs.
Fry paid numerous visits, arranging for the
instruction, employment, and cleanliness of the
women. A worthy fellow-helper, Mrs. Pryor,
was her companion, on most of these journeys,
frequently enduring exposure to weather, rough
seas, and accidents. On one occasion the two
sisters of mercy ran the risk of drowning, but
were fortunately rescued by a passing vessel.
Very fortunate, indeed, was it, that a deliverer
was at hand, or the little boat, toiling up the
river, contending against tide, wind and weather,
might have been lost. That voyage to Grave-
send was only one among many destined to work
a revolution in female convict life.

Alterations, which were not always improvements, began to take place in the manner of receiving these women on board ship. The vessels were moored at Woolwich, and group by group the miserable complement of passengers arrived; in each case, however, controlled by male warders. Sometimes, a turnkey would bring his party on the outside of a stage-coach; another might bring a contingent in a smack, or coasting vessel; while yet a third marched up a band of heavily-ironed women, whose dialects told from which districts they came. Sometimes their infants were left behind, and, in such a case, one of the ladies would go to Whitehall to obtain the necessary order to enable the unfortunate nursling to accompany its mother; but generally speaking, the children accompanied and shared the parents' fortunes.

Cruelties were inseparable from the customs which prevailed. In 1822, Mrs. Pryor discovered that prisoners from Lancaster Castle arrived, not merely handcuffed, but with heavy irons on their legs, which had occasioned considerable swelling, and in one instance serious inflammation. *The Brothers* sailed in 1823, with its freight of human misery on board, and the suffering which resulted from the mode of ironing was so great, that Mrs. Fry took down the names and particulars, in order to make representations to the Government. Twelve women arrived on board the vessel, handcuffed ; eleven others had iron hoops round their legs and arms, and were chained to each other. The complaints of these women were mournful; they were not allowed to get up or down from the coach, without the whole party being dragged together; some of them had children to carry, but they received no help, no alleviation to their sufferings. One woman from Wales must have had a bitter experience of irons. She came to the ship with a hoop around her ankle, and when the sub-matron insisted on having it removed, the operation was so painful that the poor wretch fainted. She told Mrs. Fry that she had worn, for some time, an iron hoop around her waist ; from that, a chain connected with hoops round her legs above the knee ; from these, another chain was fastened to irons round her ankles. Not content with this, her hands were confined *every night* to the hoop which went round her waist, while she lay like a log on her bed of straw. Such tales remind one of the tortures of the Inquisition.

The "Newgate women" were especially noticeable for good conduct on the voyage out. Their conduct was reported to be "exemplary" by the Surgeon Superintendent, and their industry was most pleasing. Their patchwork was highly prized by many, and indeed treasured up by some of them for many years after. Officers in the British navy assisted in the good work by word and deed ; in fact, Captain Young, of Deptford Dockyard, first suggested the making of patchwork as an employment on board ship. From some correspondence which passed between Mrs. Fry and the Controller of the Navy, in 1820, we find that the building for the women in New South Wales was begun ; while in a letter written about this time to a member of the Government, she explains her desires and plans relative to the female convicts after their arrival at Hobart Town, Tasmania.

This letter is full of interesting points. After noticing the fact of the building at Hobart Town being imperatively needed, she goes on to suggest that a respectable and judicious matron should be stationed in that building, responsible, under the Governor and magistrates, for the order of the inmates ; that part of the building should be devoted to school purposes ; that immediately on the arrival of a ship, a Government Inspector should visit the vessel and report ; that the Surgeon Superintendent should have a description of each woman's offense, character, and capability, so that her disposal in the colony might be made in a little less hap-hazard fashion than hitherto ; that the best behaved should be taken into domestic service by such of the residents of the colony as chose to coöperate, while the others should remain at the Home, under prison rules, until they have earned the privilege of going to service ; and that a sufficient supply of serviceable clothing should be provided. She further recommended the adoption of a uniform dress for the convicts, as conducive to order and discipline, and, as a last and indispensable condition, the appointment of a matron, in order to enforce needful regulations. This epistle was sent with the prayer that Earl Bathurst would peruse it, and grant the requests of the writer. It is refreshing to be able to add that red tapeism did not interfere with the adoption of these suggestions, but that they met with prompt consideration.

Every year, four, five, or six convict-ships went out to the colonies of Australia with their burdens of sin, sorrow and guilt. Van Diemen's Land and New South Wales received annually fresh consignments of the outcast iniquity of the Old World. Mrs. Fry made a point of visiting each ship before it sailed, as many times as her numerous duties permitted, and bade the convicts most affectionate and anxious farewells. These good-bye visits were alway semi-religious ones; without her Bible and the teaching which pointed to a better life beyond, Mrs. Fry would have been helpless to cope with the vice and misery which surged up before her. As it was, her heart sometimes grew faint and weary in the work, though not by any means weary of it. As an apostle of mercy to the well-nigh lost, she moved in and out among those sin-stricken companies.

Captain (afterwards Admiral) Young, Principal Resident Agent of Transports on the river Thames, forwarded the good work by every possible means. From the pen of one of the members of his family, we have a vivid picture of one of these leave-takings. It occurred on board a vessel lying off Woolwich, in 1826. William Wilberforce, of anti-slavery fame, and several other friends, accompanied the party. This chronicler writes : —

On board one of them [there were two convict ships lying in the river] between two and three hundred women were assembled, in order to listen to the exhortations and prayers of perhaps the two brightest personifications of Christian philanthropy that the age could boast. Scarcely could two voices even so distinguished for beauty and power be imagined united in a more touching engagement; as, indeed, was testified by the breathless attention, the tears and suppressed sobs of the gathered listeners. No lapse of time can ever efface the impression of the 107th Psalm, as read by Mrs. Fry with such extraordinary emphasis and intonation, that it seemed to make the simple reading a commentary.

We find in the annals of her life the particulars of another visit to the *George Hibbert* convict-ship, in 1734. She had, about this time, pleaded earnestly with Lord Melbourne, the Home Secretary, for the appointment of matrons to these vessels. She records gratefully the fact, that both his lordship and Mr. Spring Rice received her "in the handsomest manner," giving her a most patient and appreciative hearing. She succeeded at this time in obtaining a part of the boon which she craved. Mrs. Saunders, the wife of a missionary returning to the colony, was permitted by the Government to fill the office of matron to the convicts. For this service, Government gave the lady a free passage. There was double advantage in this, because, when by reason of sea-sickness, Mrs. Saunders felt ill, Mr. Saunders occupied her place as far as possible, and performed the duties of chaplain and school-master. The Ladies' British Society, formed by Mrs. Fry, for the superintendence of this and other good works relating to convicts and prisons, united in promoting the appointment of this worthy couple, and were highly gratified at the result of the experiment; as appears by extracts from the books of the Convict Ship Committee.

Finally, when the voyage was ended, the Surgeon Superintendent gave good-conduct tickets to all whose behavior had been satisfactory, and secured them engagements in respectable situations. Better than all, there was a proper building which ensured shelter, classification, and restraint. The horrors of the outcast life, so vividly described by Mr. Marsden in his letter from Paramatta, no longer existed. The work of these ladies, uphill though it had been, was now bearing manifold fruit. And the results of this more humane and rational system of treatment upon the future of the colonies themselves could not but appear in time. There were on board this very vessel, the *George Hibbert*, 150 female convicts, with forty-one children ; also nine free women, carrying with them twenty-three young children, who were going out to their husbands who had been transported previously. When it is remembered that these people were laying the foundations of new colonies, and peopling them with their descendants, it must be conceded that in her efforts to humanize and christianize them, Mrs. Fry's far-reaching philanthropy became a great national benefit. With modest thankfulness, she herself records, after an interview with Queen Adelaide and some of the royal family, " Surely, the result of our labors has hitherto been beyond our most sanguine expectations, as to the improved state of our prisons, female convict-ships, and the convicts in New South Wales."

CHAPTER X.

CONTRARY to the general practice of mankind
in matters of pure benevolence, Mrs. Fry looked
around for new worlds to conquer, in the shape
of yet unfathomed prison miseries. Many, if
not most people, would have rested upon the
laurels already won, and have been contented
with the measures of good already achieved.
Not so with the philanthropist whose work we
sketch. Like an ever-widening stream, her
life rolled on, full of acts of mercy, growing
wider and broader in its channel of operations
and its schemes of mercy. In pursuance of
these schemes she visited prisons at Nottingham, Lincoln, Wakefield, Leeds, Doncaster,
Sheffield, York, Durham, Newcastle, Carlisle,
Lancaster, Liverpool, and most other towns of
any size in England. She extended these journeys, at different times, into Scotland and Ireland, examining into the condition of prisons
and prisoners with the deepest interest. It was
her usual custom to form ladies' prison-visiting

societies, wherever practicable, and to communicate to the authorities subsequently her
views and suggestions in letters, dealing with
these matters in detail.

But her fame was not confined within the
limits of the British Isles. Communications
reached her from St. Petersburg, from Ham-
burg, from Brussels, from Baden, from Paris,
Berlin, and Potsdam ; all tending to show that
enquiry was abroad, that nations and governments as well as individuals were waking up to
a sense of their responsibilities. Both rulers
and legislators were beginning to see that *preventing* crime was wiser than *punishing* it, that
the reformation of the criminal classes was the
great end of punitive measures. This conviction reached, it was comparatively easy for the
philanthropists to work.

Before proceeding to the Continent, however,
we find notes of one or two very interesting
visits to the Channel Isles. Her first visit was
made in 1833, and, to her surprise, she found
that the islands had most thoroughly ignored
the prison teachings and improvements which
had been gaining so much ground in the United
Kingdom. The reason of this was not far to
seek. Acts of ˙Parliament passed in England
had no power in the Channel Isles ; as part of
the old Duchy of Normandy, they were governed

by their own laws and customs. The inhabitants, in their appearance, manners, language,
and usages, resemble the French more than they
do the English. Nothing deterred, however,
Mrs. Fry made a tour of inspection, and then
according to her custom sent the result of her
inquiries, and the conclusions at which she had
arrived, in the form of a letter to the authorities. That letter is far too long for reproduction
in extenso, but a few of its leading recommendations were :—

1st. A full sufficiency of employment, proportioned to
the age, sex, health and ability of each prisoner.

2d. A proper system of classification, including the
separation of men from women, of tried from untried
prisoners, and of debtors from criminals.

3d. A fixed and suitable dietary for criminals, together
with an absolute prohibition of intoxicating drinks.

4th. A suitable prison dress with distinctive badges.

5th. A complete code of regulations binding on all
officials.

6th. The appointment of a visiting committee to inspect
the prison regularly and frequently.

7th. Provision to be made for the instruction of criminals in the common branches of education, and for the
performance of divine service at stated seasons by an
appointed chaplain.

After adverting to the fact that the island
was independent of British control, she alluded
to "the progressive wisdom of the age" in

respect to prison discipline and management, and urged the authorities to be abreast of the times in adopting palliative measures. The whole penal system of the islands required to be renewed, and it promised to be a work of time before this could be effected. We find that Mrs. Fry exerted herself for many years to this end; but it was not until after the lapse of years, and after two visits to the islands, that she succeeded.

The hospital at Jersey seemed to be a curious sort of institution designed to shelter destitute sick and poor, as well as to secure the persons of small offenders, and lunatics. Punishment with fetters was inflicted in this place upon all those who tried to escape, so that it was a sort of prison. Mrs. Fry's quick eye detected many abuses in its management, and her pen suggested remedies for them.

At Guernsey, the same irregularities and abuses appeared, and were attacked in her characteristic manner. In both these islands, as well as in Sark, she inaugurated works of charity and religion, thus sowing imperishable seed destined to bear untold fruit. Finally, after more visits from herself, and special inspectors appointed by Government, a new house of correction was built in Jersey, while other improvements necessary to the working out of her prison system were, one by one, adopted.

In January, 1838, she paid her first visit to
France, being accompanied on this journey by
her husband, by Josiah Forster, and by Lydia
Irving, members of the Society of Friends.
True to her instinct, she found her way speedily
into the prisons of the French capital, examin-
ing, criticising, recommending and teaching.
She could not speak much French, but some
kind friend always interpreted her observations.
From her journal it seems that solemn prayer
for Divine guidance and blessing occupied the
forenoon of the first day in Paris ; after that,
visits of ceremony were paid to the English
Ambassador, and of friendship to other persons.
Among the prisons visited were the St. Lazare
Prison for women, containing 952 inmates, La
Force Prison for men, the Central Prison at
Poissy, and that of the Conciergerie. The first-
named, that of St. Lazare, was visited several
times, and portions of Scripture read, as at Newgate. The listeners were very much affected,
manifesting their feelings by frequent exclama-
tions and tears. Lady Granville, Lady Georgina
Fullerton, and some other ladies accompanied
Mrs. Fry to this prison on one visit, when
all agreed that much good would result from
the appointment and work of a Ladies' Committee. Hospitals, schools, and convents also
came in for a share of attention ; and after dis-

cussing points of interest connected with the
prisons with the Prefect of Police, she concluded by obtaining audience of the King, Queen
and Duchess of Orleans.

On the journey homeward the party visited
the prisons of Caen, Rouen and Beaulieu, distributing copies of the Scriptures to the prisoners.   She notices with much delight the united
feeling in respect of benevolent objects which
existed between Roman Catholics and herself.
Her own words are "a hidden power of good at
work amongst them ; many very extraordinary
Christian characters, bright, sober, zealous
Roman Catholics and Protestants."

In the commencement of 1839, the low state
of the funds of the different benevolent societies formed in connection with her prison
labors, exercised her faith.   None ever carried
into practice more fully the old monkish maxim
Laborare est orare.   Refuges had been formed, at
Chelsea for girls, and at Clapham for women,
while the Ladies' Society and the convict-ships
demanded funds incessantly.   A fancy sale was
held in Crosby Hall, "conducted in a sober,
quiet manner," which realized over a thousand
pounds for these charities.   After recording the
fact with thankfulness, Mrs. Fry paid her
second visit to the Continent, going as far as
Switzerland on her errand of mercy.

At Paris she was received affectionately by those friends who had listened to her voice on her previous visit. Baron de Gerando and other philanthropists gathered around her, oblivious of the distinctions of creeds and churches, and bent only on accomplishing a successful crusade against vice and misery.

Among the hospitals inspected by her were the hospital of St. Louis for the plague, leprosy, and other infectious disorders; the Hospice de la Maternité, and the Hospice des Enfans Trouvés. This latter was founded by St. Vincent de Paul for the bringing up of foundlings, but had fallen into a state of pitiable neglect. From the un-natural treatment which these poor waifs received, the mortality had reached a frightful pitch. It seemed, from Mrs. Fry's statements, that the little creatures were bound up for hours together, being only released from their "swad-dlings" once in every twelve hours for any and every purpose. The sound in the wards could only be compared to the faint and pitiful bleat-ing of lambs. A lady who frequently visited the institution said that she never remembered examining the array of clean white cots that lined the walls without finding at least one dead babe. "In front of the fire was a sloping stage, on which was a mattress, and a row of these little creatures placed on it to warm and await

their turn to be fed from the spoon by a nurse.
After much persuasion, one that was crying
piteously was released from its swaddling bands ;
it stretched its little limbs, and ceased its wail-
ings." Supposing these children of misfortune
survived the first few weeks of such a life they
were sent into the country to be reared by
different peasants ; but there again a large per
centage died from infantile diseases.   Mrs. Fry
succeeded in securing some ameliorations of the
treatment of the babes ; but sisters, doctors,
superior, and all, seemed bound by the iron
bands of custom and tradition.

The Archbishop of Paris was somewhat annoyed at her proceedings and expressed his
displeasure ; it seemed more, however, to be
directed against her practice of distributing the
Scriptures, than really against her prison work.

At Nismes, under the escort of five armed
soldiers, because of the known violence of the
desperadoes whom she visited, she inspected
the Maison Centrale, containing about 1,200
prisoners.   She interceded for some of them
that they might be released from their fetters,
undertaking at the same time that the released
prisoners should behave well.   At a subsequent
visit, after holding a religious service among
these felons, the same men thanked her with
tears of gratitude.

Much to her delight, she discovered a body of religionists who held principles similar to those of the Society of Friends. They were descendants of the Camisards, a sect of Protestants who took refuge in the mountains of the Cevennes during the persecution which followed the revocation of the Edict of Nantes, and were descended originally from the Albigenses. Their three most distinguished pastors were Claude Brousson, who took part in the sufferings at the general persecution of the Protestants; Jean Cavalier, the soldier-pastor who led his flock to battle, and who now sleeps in an English graveyard; and Antoine Court, who formed this "church in the desert," into a more compact body. The first of these pastors was hanged for "heresy" at Montpellier, in 1698; but he, together with his successors, labored so devoutly and so ardently, that the persecuted remnant rose from the dust and proved themselves valiant for the truth as they had received and believed it. It was not possible that the seed of a people which had learnt the sermons preached to them off by heart, and written the texts on stone tablets, in order to pass them from one mountain village to another, could ever die out. The descendants of those martyrs had come down through long generations, to flourish at last openly in Nismes. Mrs. Fry recognized in them the kindred souls of faithful believers. After this, the party spent a fortnight at a little retired village called Congenies, where they welcomed many others of their own creed. A house with "vaulted rooms, whitewashed and floored with stone," sheltered them during this quaint sojourn, while the villagers vied with each other in contributing to their comforts.

At Toulon they visited the "Bagnes," or prison for the galley slaves. These poor wretches fared horribly, while the loss of life among them was terrible. They worked very hard, slept on boards, and were fed upon bread and dry beans. At night they were ranged in a long gallery, and in number from one hundred to two hundred, were all chained to the iron rod which ran the entire length of the gallery. By day they worked chained together in couples.

At Marseilles a new kind of prison was inspected by her ; this was a conventual institution and refuge for female penitents, under the control of the nuns of the order of St. Charles, who to the three ordinary vows of poverty, chastity, and obedience, added that of converting souls. Superintending ladies in the city, who bore the title of "directresses," were not even permitted to see the women immured there ; indeed, only one was permitted to enter the building in order to look after the necessary repairs, and even she was strictly restrained from seeing a penitent or sister. It seemed hopeless in the face of these facts to expect admission, but Mrs. Fry's name and errand prevailed. Accompanied by one of these nominal directresses, she was admitted and shown into a large, plainly-furnished parlor. After she had waited some little time, the Lady Superior presented herself at the grating, and prepared to hear the communications of her visitors. In the course of the conversation which passed, it appeared that there were over one hundred penitents in the convent, who mostly became servants after their reclamation. It seemed that they "were not taught to read or write, neither was the least morsel of pencil, paper, pen, ink, or any other possible material for writing permitted, from the fear of their communicating with people without." The Superior admitted that portions of the Bible were suitable to the inmates, such as the Parables and Psalms, but said that as a whole the Scriptures were not fit to be put into the hands of people in general. Mrs. Fry departed from this "home of mystery and darkness," very unsatisfied and sad. She next visited a boys' prison, conducted by the Abbé Fisceaux, which excited her admiration.

At the "Maison Pénitentiaire" at Geneva, the arrangements appeared to be as complete as possible, and most praiseworthy. The treatment varied in severity, according to the guilt of the criminals, who were divided into four classes. They were in all cases there for long terms of imprisonment, but were allowed either Catholic or Protestant versions of the Scriptures, according to their faith. After paying short visits to Lausanne, Berne, and Zurich, the party returned home.

As her life passed on and infirmities grew apace, it seemed that Mrs. Fry's zeal and charity grew also, for she planned and schemed to do good with never-flagging delight. Early in 1840, she departed again for the Continent, accompanied this time by her brother, Samuel Gurney, and his daughter, by William Allen and Lucy Bradshaw. During this journey and a subsequent one, she had much intercourse with royal and noble personages. At Brussels they had a pleasant audience of the King, who held an interesting conversation with them on the state of Belgian prisons. A large prison for boys at Antwerp specially drew forth their commendations ; it seemed admirably arranged and conducted, while every provision was made for the instruction and improvement of the lads. At Hameln, in Hanover, they found one of the opposite class, a men's prison, containing about four hundred inmates, but all heavily chained " to the ground, until they would confess their crimes, whether they had committed them or not." One wonders if this treatment still prevails in the Hameln of Robert Browning's ballad. At Hanover they waited on the Queen by special command, and during a long interview many interesting and important subjects were brought forward.

At Berlin they were received by royalty in the most cordial way. Mrs. Fry's niece, in a letter, gives a vivid account of the assembly at the royal palace specially invited to meet the Quakeress and her party.

The Princess William has been very desirous to give her sanction, as far as possible, to the Ladies' Committee for visiting the prison, that my aunt had been forming; and, to show her full approbation, had invited the Committee to meet her at her palace. So imagine about twenty ladies assembling here, at our hotel, at half-past twelve o'clock to-day, beautifully dressed; and, further fancy us all driving off and arriving at the palace. The Princess had also asked some of her friends, so we must have numbered about forty. Such a party of ladies, and only our friend Count Gröben to interpret. The Princess received us most kindly, and conducted us herself to the top of the room; we talked some time, whilst awaiting the arrival of other members of the royal family. The ladies walked about the suite of rooms for about half an hour, taking chocolate, and waiting for the Crown Princess, who soon arrived. The Princess Charles was also there, and the Crown Prince himself soon afterwards entered. I could not but long for a painter's eye to have carried away the scene. All of us

seated in that beautiful room, our aunt in the middle of
the sofa, the Crown Prince and Princess and the Princess Charles on her right; the Princess William, the
Princess Marie, and the Princess Czartoryski on the left;
Count Gröben sitting near her to interpret, the Countesses
Böhlem and Dernath by her. I was sitting by the Countess Schlieffen, a delightful person, who is much interested in all our proceedings. A table was placed before
our aunt, with pens, ink, and paper, like other committees, with the various rules our aunt and I had drawn up,
and the Countess Böhlem had translated into German,
and which she read to the assembly. After that my
aunt gave a concise account of the societies in England,
commencing every fresh sentence with " If the Prince
and Princesses will permit." When business was over,
my aunt mentioned some texts, which she asked leave to
read. A German Bible was handed to Count Gröben,
the text in Isaiah having been pointed out that our good
aunt had wished for, " Is not this the fast that I have
chosen," etc. The Count read it, after which our aunt
said, " Will the Prince and Princesses allow a short time
for prayer?" They all bowed assent and stood, while
she knelt down and offered one of her touching, heart-
felt prayers for them — that a blessing might rest on the
whole place, from the King on his throne to the poor
prisoner in the dungeon; and she prayed especially for
the royal family; then for the ladies, that the works of
their hands might be prospered in what they had undertaken to perform. Many of the ladies now withdrew,
and we were soon left with the royal family. They all
invited us to see them again, before we left Berlin, and
took leave of us in the kindest manner.

One result of the reception accorded Mrs.
Fry by royalty was the amelioration of the con-

dition of the Lutherans. It came about in this way: in the course of her inquiries and inter- course among the people of the Prussian dominions, she discovered that adherents to the Lutheran Church were subject to much petty persecution on behalf of their faith. True they were not dealt with so cruelly as in former times, but frequently, at that very day, they were imprisoned, or suffered the loss of property because of their religious opinions. The mat- ter lay heavily on Mrs. Fry's benevolent heart, and, seizing the opportunity, she spoke to the Crown Prince at the meeting just described, on the behalf of the persecuted Christians. The Crown Prince listened most attentively, and advised her to lay the matter before the King in any way she deemed proper. A petition was therefore drawn up by William Allen, translated into German, and with much fear and trembling presented to His Majesty. The following day the King's chaplain was sent bearing the "de- lightful intelligence" that the petition had been received; further, the King had said that "he thought the Spirit of God must have helped them to express themselves as they had done."

About this time we find the following entry in her journal : "I have been poorly enough to have the end of life brought closely before me, and to stimulate me in faith to do *quickly* what

my Lord may require me." Accordingly, engagements and undertakings multiplied, and
1841 witnessed another brief visit to the continent of Europe. She seemed more and more
to get the conviction that she must lose no time
while about her Master's business, and such her
prison, asylum and hospital labors most assur-
edly were. The shadows of life's evening were
gathering around her, and heart and flesh beginning to fail, but no efforts of charity or
mercy might be found lacking.

On this visit her brother, Joseph John
Gurney, and two nieces accompanied her.
Soon after arriving at the Hague, Mrs. Fry and
Mr. Gurney, being introduced to the King by
Prince Albert, were commanded to attend at a
royal audience. This the travellers did, and,
after about an hour's conversation, departed
highly gratified. Another day they spent some
time with the Princess of Orange, the Princess
Frederick, and other members of the royal
house : all these personages were anxious to
hear about the work of prison reform, and to
aid in it. After this they departed for Amster-
dam, Bremen, and other places; but their journey resembled a triumphal progress more than
anything else. The peasantry followed the
carriage shouting Mrs. Fry's name, and begging for tracts. Sometimes, in order to get

away, she was compelled to shake hands with them all, and speak a few words of kindly greeting.

They extended the journey into Denmark, and were treated with marked honor from the first. The Queen engaged apartments for the travellers at the Hotel Royal, and on some occasions took Mrs. Fry to see schools and other places, in her own carriage. On a subsequent day, when dining with the King and Queen, Mrs. Fry and Mr. Gurney laid before their Majesties the condition of persecuted Christians ; the sad state of prisons in his dominions ; they also referred to the slavery in the Danish colonies in the West Indies. Mr. Gurney having only recently returned from that part of the world, he had much to tell respecting the spiritual and social state of those colonies. Mrs. Fry records that at dinner she was placed between the King and Queen, who both conversed very pleasantly with her.

At Minden, they had varied experiences of travelling and travellers' welcomes. " I could not but be struck," says Mrs. Fry in her journal, "with the peculiar contrast of my circumstances : in the morning traversing the bad pavement of a street in Minden, with a poor old Friend in a sort of knitted cap close to her head ; in the evening surrounded by the Prince and Princesses of a German Court." The members of the Prussian royal family were anxious to see her and hear from her own lips an account of her labors in the cause of humanity. The representatives of the House of Brandenburgh welcomed Mrs. Fry beyond her most sanguine expectations ; indeed, it would be nearer the truth to say that in her lowly estimate of herself, she almost dreaded to approach royal or noble personages, and that therefore she craved for no honor, but only tolerance and favor. She never sought an interview with any of these personages, but to benefit those who could not plead for themselves. Her letters home exhibit no pride, boastfulness, or triumph ; all is pure thankfulness that one so unworthy as she deemed herself to be should accomplish so much. Writing to her grandchildren she says :

"We dined at the Princess William's with several of the royal family. The Queen came afterwards and appeared much pleased at my delight on hearing that the King had stopped religious persecutions in the country, and that several other things had been improved since our last visit. It is a very great comfort to believe that our efforts for the good of others have been blessed. Yesterday we paid a very interesting visit to the Queen, then to Prince Frederick of Holland and his Princess, sister to the King of Prussia; with her we had much serious conversation upon many important subjects, as

we also had with the Queen. . . . . Although looked up
to by all, they appear so humble, so moderate in everything. I think the Christian ladies on the Continent
dress far more simply than those in England. The
Countess appeared very liberal, but extravagant in nothing. To please us she had apple dumplings, which were
quite a curiosity; they were really very nice. The company stood still before and after dinner, instead of saying
grace. We returned from our interesting meeting at the
Countess's, about eleven o'clock in the evening. The
royal family were assembled and numbers of the nobility;
after a while the King and Queen arrived; the poor Tyrolese flocked in numbers. I doubt such a meeting ever
having been held anywhere before, — the curious mixture
of all ranks and conditions. My poor heart almost failed
me. Most earnestly did I pray for best help, and not
unduly to fear man. The royal family sat together,
or nearly so; the King and Queen, Princess William,
and Princess Frederick, Princess Mary, Prince William,
Prince Charles, Prince Frederick of the Netherlands,
young Prince William, besides several other princes
and princesses not royal. Your uncle Joseph spoke
for a little while, explaining our views on worship.
Then I enlarged upon the changes that had taken place
since I was last in Prussia; mentioned the late King's
kindness to these poor Tyrolese in their affliction and
distress; afterwards addressed these poor people, and
then those of high rank, and felt greatly helped to speak
the truth to them in love. They finished with a hymn."

Her last brief visit to the Continent was paid
in 1843, and spent wholly in Paris. Mrs. Fry
was particularly interested in French prisons,
as well as in the measures designed to amelio-

rate the condition of those who tenanted them.
Reformation had become the order of the day
there as in England; the Duchess of Orleans,
the Grand Duchess of Mecklenburg, M. Guizot,
the Duc de Broglie, M. de Tocqueville, M. Car-
not, and other high and noble personages were
much interested in the subject. A bill to sanction the needful reforms was introduced to the
Chamber of Deputies by the Minister of the
Interior, and ably supported by him in a speech
of great lucidity and power. Said he, when laying it before the Chamber: "Our subject is
not entirely to sequestrate the prisoner nor to
confine him to absolute solitude. Some of the
provisions of the bill will mitigate the principle
of solitary confinement in a manner which was
suggested by the Commission of 1840, and
should not pass unnoticed by the Chamber.
Convicts sentenced to more than twelve years'
hard labor, or to perpetual hard labor, after having gone through twelve years of their punishment, or when they shall have attained the age
of seventy, will be no longer separated from
others, except during the night." The bill
further provided, besides this mitigation of the
solitary confinement system, that the "Bagnes,"
where galley slaves had hitherto labored, should
be replaced by houses of hard labor, and that
smaller prisons should be erected for minor

offenses instead of sending criminals convicted
of them to the great central prisons. The bill
was certainly destined to effect a total revolution in the management of such places as St.
Lazare and similar prisons, in addition to giving
solid promise of improvement in the punitive
system of France.

During this brief final visit to the French
capital, Mrs. Fry entered on her sixty-third
year, aged and infirm in body, but still animated
by the master passion of serving the sad and
sorrowful. Her brother, Joseph John Gurney,
together with his wife, were with her in Paris,
but they pursued their journey into Switzerland, while she returned home in June, feeling
that life's shadows were lengthening apace, and
that not much time remained to her in which
to complete her work. The impressions she
had made on the society of the gay city had
been altogether good. Like the people who
stared at the pilgrims passing through Vanity
Fair, the Parisians wondered, and understood
for the first time that here was a lady who did
indeed pass through things temporal, "with
eyes fixed on things eternal"; and whose
supreme delight lay, not in ball-rooms, race-
courses, or courts, but in finding out suffering
humanity and striving to alleviate its woes.
Doubtless many of the gay Parisians shrugged

their shoulders and smiled good-humoredly at
the "illusion," "notion," "fanaticism," or
whatever else they called it ; they were simply
living on too low a plane of life to understand,
or to criticise Mrs. Fry. Except animated by
somewhat of fellow-feeling, none can understand
her career even now. It stands too far apart
from, too highly lifted above, our ordinary pursuits and pleasures, to be compared with anything that less philanthropic-minded mortals
may do. It called for a far larger amount of
self-denial than ordinary people are capable of ;
it demanded too much singleness of purpose
and sincerity of speech. Had Mrs. Fry not
come from a Quaker stock she might have con-
formed more to the ways and manners of
fashionable society ; had she possessed less of
sterling piety, she might have sought to serve
her fellow-creatures in more easy paths. As a
reformer, she was sometimes misunderstood,
abused, and spoken evil of. It was always the
case and always will be, that reformers receive
injustice. Only, in some cases, as in this one,
time reverses the injustice, and metes out due
honor. As a consequence, Elizabeth Fry's
name is surrounded with an aureola of fame,
and her self-abnegation affords a sublime spectacle to thoughtful minds of all creeds and
classes ; for, simply doing good is seen to be
the highest glory.

CHAPTER XI.

NEW THEORIES OF PRISON DISCIPLINE AND MANAGEMENT.

Mrs. Fry's opinions on prison discipline and management were necessarily much opposed to those which had obtained prior to her day. No one who has followed her career attentively, can fail to perceive that her course of prison management was based upon well arranged and carefully worked out principles. In various letters, in evidence before committees of both Houses of Parliament, and in private intercourse, Mrs. Fry made these principles and rules as fully known and as widely proclaimed as it was possible to do. But, like all reformers, she felt the need of securing a wider dissemination of them. Evidence given before committees, was, in many points, deferred to ; private suggestions and recommendations were frequently adopted, but a large class of inquirers were too far from the sphere of her influence to be moved in this way. For the sake of these, and the general public, she deemed it

wise to embody her opinions and rules in a
treatise, which gives in small compass, but very
clearly, the *rationale* of her treatment of prisoners ; and lays down suggestions, hints, and
principles upon which others could work.
Within about seventy octavo pages, she dis-
courses practically and plainly on the formation
of Ladies' Committees for visiting prisons, on
the right method of proceeding in a prison after
the formation of such a committee, on female
officers in prisons, on separate prisons for
females, on inspection and classification, on
instruction and employment, on medical attendance, diet, and clothing, and on benevolent
efforts for prisoners who have served their sentences. It is easy to recognize in these pages
the Quakeress, the woman, and the Christian.
She recommends to the attention of ladies, as
departments for doing good, not only prisons,
but lunatic asylums, hospitals and workhouses.
At the same time she strongly recommends
that only *orderly* and *experienced* visitors should
endeavor to penetrate into the abodes of vice
and wickedness, which the prisons of England at
that day mostly were. Among other judicious
counsels for the conduct of these visitors occur
the following, which read as coming from her
own experience. That this was the case we may
feel assured ; Mrs. Fry was too wise and too

womanly not to warn others from the pit-falls over which she had stumbled, or to permit any-one to fall into her early mistakes :—

" Much depends on the spirit in which the worker enters upon her work. It must be the spirit not of judgment but of mercy. She must not say in her heart, 'I am holier than thou'; but must rather keep in perpetual remembrance that '*all* have sinned,' and that, therefore, great pity is due from us even to the greatest transgressors among our fellow-creatures, and that in meekness and love we ought to labor for their restoration. The good principle in the hearts of many abandoned persons may be compared to the few remaining sparks of a nearly extinguished fire. By means of the utmost care and attention, united with the most gentle treatment, these may yet be fanned into a flame; but under the operation of a rough and violent hand they will presently disappear and be lost forever. In our conduct with these unfortunate females, kindness, gentleness, and true humility ought ever to be united with serenity and firmness. Nor will it be safe ever to descend, in our intercourse with them, to *familiarity*, for there is a dignity in the Christian character which demands, and will obtain, respect; and which is power-ful in its influence even over dissolute minds. . . . Neither is it by any means wise to converse with them on the subject of the crimes of which they are accused or convicted, for such conversation is injurious both to the criminals themselves and to others who hear them; and, moreover, too frequently leads them to add sin to sin, by uttering the grossest falsehoods. And those who engage in the interesting task of visiting crimi-nals must not be impatient if they find the work of reformation a very slow one. . . . Much disadvantage will accrue generally from endeavors on the part of visiting ladies to procure the mitigation of the sentences of criminals. Such endeavors ought never to be made except where the cases are remarkably clear, and then through the official channels. Deeply as we must deplore the baneful effects of the punishment of death, and painful as we must feel it to be that our fellow-creatures, in whose welfare we are interested, should be prematurely plunged into an awful eternity, yet, while our laws continue as they are, unless they can bring forward *decided facts* in favor of the condemned, it is wiser for the visiting ladies to be quiet, and to submit to decrees which they cannot alter."

In reference to the choice of officers, she strongly insists that all officers — superior and inferior — shall be females. She prefers a widow for the post of matron, because of her superior knowledge of the world and of life; and never should she or her subordinates be chosen "because the situation is suited to their wants, but because they are suited to fill the situation." She holds it of the first importance that the matrons should not only be of a superior station in life, but that they should be decidedly religious. This little book was written in 1827, but from her insistence upon this as a first requisite in proper dealing with female prisoners, it appears likely that the then recent act of George IV., had not been commonly complied with. This act provides that a "matron shall be appointed in every prison in which female prisoners shall be confined, who shall reside in the prison ; and it shall be the duty of the matron constantly to superintend the female prisoners." Again, another clause of the Act says, " Females shall in all cases be attended by female officers." That these provisions had only been partially carried out, is proved by her words relative to this clause : " Since the passing of the late Act of Parliament for the regulations of prisons, our large jails have been generally provided with a matron and female turnkeys ; but it is much to be regretted that in many smaller prisons no such provisions have yet been adopted. Nor ought it to be concealed that the persons selected to fill the office of matron are, in various instances, unsuited to their posts ; and in other cases are unfitted for its fulfillment, by residing out of prison."

With respect to the classification of prisoners, Mrs. Fry recommends four classes or divisions which should comprise the total: — 1st. Prisoners of previous good character, and guilty only of venial crimes. This class, she suggests, should be allowed to dress a little better and be put to lighter labors than the others. From their ranks, also, should temporary officers be selected, while small pecuniary rewards might be with propriety offered. 2d. Prisoners con-

victed of more serious crimes. These should
be treated with more strictness ; but it should
be possible for a prisoner, by constant good conduct and obedience to rules, to rise into the first
class. 3d. In this class the privileges were to
be considerably diminished, while the 4th class
consisted only of hardened offenders, guilty of
serious crimes, and of those who had been frequently committed. " This class must undergo
its peculiar privations and hardships." Still,
that hope may not entirely give place to despair,
Mrs. Fry recommends that even these criminals
should be eligible for promotion to the upper
classes upon good behavior. It will be seen that
this system partook somewhat of Captain
Machonochie's merit, or good-mark system,
introduced by him with such remarkable success into Norfolk Island.

Among other suggestions relative to the classification of prisoners we find one recommending the wearing of a ticket by each woman.
Every ticket was to be inscribed with a number, which number should agree with the corresponding number on the class list. Each class
list was to be kept by the matron or visitors,
and was to include a register of the conduct of
the prisoners. In the case of convicts on board
convict-ships proceeding to the penal settlements, Mrs. Fry recommended that not only

should the women wear these tickets, but that every article of clothing, every book, and every piece of bedding should be similarly numbered ; even the convicts' seats at table should be distinguished by the same numbers in order to prevent disputes, and to promote order and regularity.

She considered the most thorough, vigilant, and unremitting inspection essential to a correct system of prison discipline ; by this means she anticipated that an effectual, if slow, change of habits might be produced.

With regard to the instruction of prisoners, she held decided views as to the primary importance of Scriptural knowledge. The Bible, and the Bible alone, was to be the text-book for this purpose, while nothing sectarian was to be admitted ; but in their fullest sense, "the esssential and saving principles of our common Christianity were to be inculcated." She recommended reading, writing, arithmetic, and needlework, the last to carry with it a little remuneration, in order to afford the women some encouragement. While acknowledging the wisdom of the Act of Parliament which provided that prayers should be read daily in all prisons, she strongly urges visitors and chaplains to teach privately "that true religion and saving faith are in their nature practical, and that the reality of repentance can be proved only by good works and by an amendment in life and conversation."

For the employment of prisoners she recommends such occupations as patchwork, knitting stockings, making articles of plain needlework, washing, ironing, housework, cooking, spinning, and weaving. It should in all cases be *constant,* and in the worst cases, *disciplinary* labor. She recommends, under *strict limitations,* the treadmill for hardened, refractory, and depraved women, but only for short periods. All needleworkers especially should receive some remuneration for their work, which remuneration should be allowed to accumulate for their benefit by such time as their sentences expire, in order that when they leave prison they may possess a little money wherewith to commence the world afresh. Her words are : " The greater portion of their allotted share of earnings, however, must be reserved for them against the time of their leaving prison and returning to the world. The possession of a moderate sum of money will *then* be found of essential importance as the means of preventing an almost irresistible temptation, the temptation of want and money, to the renewal of criminal practices. And if, in laboring for this remuneration the poor criminal has also gained possession of the *habit* of industry, and has learned to appreciate the sweets of regular employment, it is more than probable that this temptation may never occur again."

Mrs. Fry quotes largely from the Act of Parliament, relative to the matters of diet, medical attendance, clothing, bedding, and firing. It seemed to be the fact that the provisions of this Act did not extend to prisons which were exclusively under local jurisdiction ; she therefore recommends lady visitors and committees to see them enforced as much as possible. While preserving even-handed justice between criminals and the country whose laws they have outraged, by suggesting that their treatment should be sufficiently penal to be humilitating, that their hair should be cut short, and all personal ornaments forbidden, she pleads earnestly for proper bedding and firing. She says : " During inclement weather, diseases are sometimes contracted by the unfortunate inmates of our jails, which can never afterwards be removed. I believe it has sometimes happened that poor creatures committed to prison for trial, have left the place of their confinement, acquitted of crime, and yet crippled for life."

From the same volume we find that Government had then inaugurated a wiser, kinder system of dealing with the convicts destined for the colonies. By the new regulations, females were allowed to take out with them all children under the age of seven years; while a mother suckling an infant was not compelled to leave England until the child was old enough to be weaned. Again, the convicts were not to be manacled in any way during their removal from the prison to the convict-ship; "but as the rule is often infringed, it is desirable that ladies of the committee should be vigilant on the subject, and should represent all cases to the governor of the prison, and afterwards, if needful, to the visiting magistrates." Further, the Government, or the boroughs, had to provide the transports with needful clothing for the voyage; and, at the end of it, the surgeon's or matron's certificate of good behavior was sufficient to ensure employment for most of the women. Altogether it seems certain that a new era for prisoners had dawned, and new ideas prevailed in regard to them. How much Mrs. Fry's labors had contributed to this state of things will never be fully known; but her work was almost accomplished.

This little book, which is a perfect *Vade Mecum* of prison management, was written in the interest of lady visitors, and for their use. It is still interesting, as showing Mrs. Fry's own mode of procedure, and the principles upon which she acted. The few quotations given in this chapter will, however, suffice for the general reader. She concludes with a pregnant sentence : " Let our prison discipline be severe in proportion to the enormity of the crimes of those on whom it is exercised, and let its strictness be such as to deter others from a similar course of iniquity, but let us ever aim at the *diminution of crime* through the just and happy medium of the REFORMATION OF CRIMINALS."

Not only in the published page, but in other ways — in fact in every possible way — did Mrs. Fry continue to proclaim the need of a new method of ordering criminals, and also of so treating them, that they should be fitted to return to society *improved* and not *degraded* by their experience of penal measures. In 1832, she was called upon to give evidence before another committee of the House of Commons, upon the best mode of enforcing " secondary punishments" so as to repress crime. On this occasion she dwelt particularly upon the points noticed in her book published five years previously, and added one or two more. For instance, while advocating complete separation at *night*, she quite as earnestly contended against what was known as the " solitary system." On this point she maintained that " solitude does not prepare women for returning to social and

domestic life, or tend so much to real improvement, as carefully arranged intercourse during
part of the day with one another under the closest superintendence and inspection, combined
with constant occupation, and solitude at night."
In her evidence there occurs the following passage : —

Every matron should live upon the spot, and be able to
inspect them closely by night and by day; and when there
are sufficient female prisoners to require it, female officers
should be appointed, and a male turnkey never permitted
to go into the women's apartments. I am convinced when
a prison is properly managed it is unnecessary, because,
by firm and gentle management, the most refractory may be
controlled by their own sex. But here I must put in a word
respecting ladies' visiting. I find a remarkable difference
depending upon whether female officers are superintended
by ladies or not. I can tell almost as soon as I go into
the prison whether they are or not, from the general
appearance both of the women and their officers. One
reason is that many of the latter are not very superior
women, not very high, either in principle or habits, and
are liable to be contaminated; they soon get familiar with
the prisoners, and cease to excite the respect due to their
office; whereas, where ladies go in once, or twice, or
three times a week, the effect produced is decided. Their
attendance keeps the female officers in their places, makes
them attend to their duty, and has a constant influence on
the minds of the prisoners themselves. In short, I may
say, after sixteen years' experience, that the result of
ladies of principle and respectability superintending the
female officers in prisons, and the prisons themselves, has

far exceeded my most sanguine expectations. In no instance have I more clearly seen the beneficial effects of ladies' visiting and superintending prisoners than on board convict-ships. I have witnessed the alterations since ladies have visited them constantly in the river. I heard formerly of the most dreadful iniquity, confusion, and frequently great distress; latterly I have seen a very wonderful improvement in their conduct. And on the voyage, I have most valuable certificates to show the difference of their condition on their arrival in the colony. I can produce, if necessary, extracts from letters. Samuel Marsden, who has been chaplain there a good many years, says it is quite a different thing: that they used to come in a most filthy, abominable state, hardly fit for any-thing; now they arrive in good order, in a totally different situation. And I have heard the same thing from others. General Darling's wife, a very valuable lady, has adopted the same system there; she has visited the prison at Paramatta, and the same thing respecting the officers is felt there as it is here. On the Continent of Europe, in various parts — St. Petersburg, Geneva, Turin, Berne, Basle, and some other places — there are corresponding societies, and the result is the same in every part. In Berlin they are doing wonders — I hear a most satisfactory account; and in St. Petersburg, where, from the barbarous state of the people, it was said it could not be done, the conduct of the prisoners has been perfectly astonishing — an entire change has been produced.

On the 22d of May, 1835, Mrs. Fry was desired to attend the Select Committee of the House of Lords, appointed to inquire into the state of the several jails and houses of correction in England and Wales. She went, accompanied by three ladies, co-workers, and escorted by Sir T. Fowell Buxton. The Duke of Richmond was chairman of the committee, which included some twelve or fifteen noblemen. An eye-witness wrote afterwards respecting Mrs. Fry's behavior and manner: "Never, should I think, was the calm dignity of her character more conspicuous. Perfectly self-possessed, her speech flowed melodiously, her ideas were clearly expressed, and if another thought possessed her besides that of delivering her opinions faithfully and judiciously upon the subjects brought before her, it was that she might speak of her Lord and Master in that noble company."

The principal topics treated of in her evidence before this committee were connected with the general state of female prisons. Among other things, she urged the want of more instruction, but that such instruction should not be given privately and *alone* to women; that the tread-mill was an undesirable punishment for women; that matrons were required to be suitable in character, age, and capability for the post; that equality in labor and diet was needed; and she insisted on the imperative necessity of Government inspectors in both Scotch and English prisons and convict-ships. She enlarged upon these matters in the manner the subject demanded, and gave the committee the impression of being in solemn earnest. Her quiet, Christian dignity impressed all who listened to her voice, while the most respectful consideration was paid to her suggestions. In reply to a question touching the instruction of the prisoners, she says : —

I believe the effect of religious and other instruction is hardly to be calculated on ; and I may further say that, notwithstanding the high estimation and reverence in which I held the Holy Scriptures, before I went to the prisons, as believing them to be written by inspiration of God, and therefore calculated to produce the greatest good, I have seen, in reading the Scripture to those women, such a power attending them, and such an effect on the minds of the most reprobate, as I could not have conceived. If anyone wants a confirmation of the truth of Christianity let him go and read the Scriptures in prison to poor sinners ; you there see how the Gospel is exactly adapted to the fallen condition of man. It has strongly confirmed my faith; and I feel it to be the bounden duty of the Government and the country that these truths shall be administered in the manner most likely to conduce to the real reformation of the prisoner. You then go to the root of the matter, for though severe punishment may in a measure deter them and others from crime, it does not amend the character and change the heart; but if you have altered the principles of the individual, they are not only deterred from crime because of the fear of punishment, but they go out, and set a bright example to others.

Both the *silent* and *solitary* systems were condemned by her as being particularly liable to abuse. She considered the silent system cruel, and especially adapted to harden the heart of a criminal even to moral petrefaction. But the strongest protest was made against *solitary* confinement. Upon every available opportunity she spoke against it to those who were in power. Unless the offense was of a very aggravated nature, she doubted the right of any man to place a fellow-creature in such misery. Some intercourse with his fellow-creatures seemed imperatively necessary if the prisoner's life and reason were to be preserved to him, and his mind to be kept from feeding upon the dark past. To dark cells she had an unconquerable aversion. Sometimes she would picture the possibility of the return of days of persecution, and urge one consideration founded upon the self-interest of the authorities themselves. "They may be building, though they little think it, dungeons for their children and their children's children if times of religious persecution or political disturbance should return." For this reason, if for no other, she urged upon those who were contemplating the erection of new prisons, the prime necessity of constructing those prisons so as to enable them to conform to the requirements of humanity.

Her opinions and reasons for and against the solitary system of confinement are well given in a communication sent to M. de Béranger after a visit to Paris, during which the subject of prison-management had formed a staple theme of discussion in the *salons* of that city. With much practical insight and clearness of reasoning, Mrs. Fry marshalled all the stock arguments, adding thereto such as her own experience taught.

In favor of the solitary system were to be urged —

1st. The prevention of all contamination by their fellow-prisoners.

2d. The impossibility of forming intimacies calculated to be injurious in after life.

3d. The increased solitude, which afforded larger opportunities for serious reflection and, if so disposed, repentance and prayer by the criminal.

4th. The prevention of total loss of character on the part of the prisoner, seeing that the *privacy* of the confinement would operate against the recognition of him by fellow-prisoners upon regaining their liberty.

Against it the following reasons could be urged : —

1st. The extreme liability to ill-treatment or indulgence, according to the mood and disposition of the officers in charge.

2d. The extreme difficulty of obtaining a

sufficiently large number of honest, high-prin-
cipled, just men and women, to carry out the
solitary system with impartiality, firmness, and,
at the same time, kindness. This reason was
strongly corroborated by the governors of Cold
Bath Fields Prison, and the great Central Prison
at Beaulieu. Their own large experience had
taught them the difficulty of securing officers in
all respects *fit to be trusted* with the administration of such a system.

3d. The very frequent result of the administration of this system by incompetent or unfit
officers would be the moral contamination of the
prisoners.

4th. The enormous expense of providing officers and accommodation sufficient to include all
the criminals of the country.

5th. The certainty of injury to body and mind
from the continuance of solitude for life. The
digestive and vocal organs, and the reason would
inevitably suffer. In proof she quoted the
notorious .imbecility of the aged monks of La
Trappe : " We are credibly informed of the fact
(in addition to what we have known at home)
that amongst the monks of La Trappe few
attain the age of sixty years without having
suffered an absolute decay of their mental powers, and fallen into premature childishness."

6th. The danger lest increased solitude instead of promoting repentance, should furnish favorable hours for the premeditation of new crimes, and so confirm the criminal in hardened sin.

7th. The impossibility of fitting the prisoners for returning to society under the system; whereas by teaching them useful employments and trades, and training them to work in company for remuneration, habits and customs may be induced which should aid in a life-long reformation.

Two or three years after the enunciation of these principles and reasons, Mrs. Fry addressed a valuable communication to Colonel Jebb in reference to the new Model Prison at Penton-ville, then (1841,) in course of construction :—

We were much interested by our visit to this new prison. We think the building generally does credit to the architect, particularly in some important points, as ventilation, the plan of the galleries, the chapel, etc., and we were also much pleased to observe the arrangement for water in each cell, and that the prisoner could ring a bell in case of wanting help.

The points that made us uneasy were, first, the dark cells, which we consider should never exist in a Christian and civilized country. I think having prisoners placed in these cells a punishment peculiarly liable to abuse. Whatever restrictions may be made for the governor of a jail, and however lenient those who *now* govern, we can little calculate upon the change the future may pro-duce, or how these very cells may one day be made use

of in case of either political or religious disturbance in
the country, or how any poor prisoner may be placed in
them in case of a more severe administration of justice.

I think no person should be placed in *total* darkness;
there should be a ray of light admitted. These cells
appear to me calculated to excite such awful terror in the
mind, not merely from their darkness but from the circumstance of their being placed within another cell, as
well as being in such a dismal situation.

I am always fearful of any punishment, beyond what
the law publicly authorizes, being privately inflicted by
any keeper or officer of a prison; for my experience
most strongly proves that there are few men who are
themselves sufficiently governed and regulated by Christian principle to be fit to have such power entrusted to
their hands; and further, I observe that officers in prisons have generally so much to try and to provoke them
that they themselves are apt to become hardened to the
more tender feelings of humanity. They necessarily also
see so much through the eyes of those under them, turnkeys and inferior officers, (too many of whom are little
removed either in education or morals from the prisoners
themselves,) that their judgments are not always just.

The next point that struck us was, that in the cells
generally the windows have that description of glass in
them that even the sight of the sky is entirely precluded.
I am aware that the motive is to prevent the possibility
of seeing a fellow-prisoner; but I think a prison for
separate confinement should be so constructed that the
culprits may at least see the sky — indeed, I should prefer more than the sky — without the liability of seeing
fellow-prisoners. My reason for this opinion is, that I
consider it a very important object to preserve the health
of mind and body in these poor creatures, and I am cer-

tain that separate confinement produces an unhealthy
state both of mind and body. Therefore everything
should be done to counteract this influence, which I am
sure is baneful in its moral tendency; for I am satisfied
that a sinful course of life increases the tendency to
mental derangement, as well as to bodily disease; and I
am as certain that an unhealthy state of mind and body
has generally a demoralizing influence; and I consider
light, air, and the power of seeing something beyond the
mere monotonous walls of a cell highly important. I am
aware that air is properly admitted, also light; still I do
think they ought to see the sky, the changes in which
make it a most pleasant object for those who are closely
confined.

When speaking of health of body and mind, I also
mean health of soul, which is ōf the first importance, for
I do not believe that a despairing or stupefied state is
suitable for leading poor sinners to a Saviour's feet for
pardon and salvation.

Mrs. Fry held quite as decided opinions upon
lunatic asylums and their keepers. It was
something terrible to her to know that poor
demented creatures lay pining, chained and ill-
treated, in dungeons; knowing no will but the
caprice of their keepers. She spared no efforts
to improve their condition; by tongue and pen
she sought to enforce new principles and modes
of action, in relation to lunatics, into the mind
of those who had to govern them. So inces-
sant were her labors to attain the ends she had
set before her, that there was not a country in

Europe which she did not influence. Almost
daily communications were coming in from
France, Denmark, Germany, Russia, Switzerland, and other countries, detailing the success
of the new plans which she had introduced and
recommended to the respective Governments.
A regular correspondence was kept up between
her and Mr. Venning of St. Petersburg, by
order of the Empress of Russia, who took the
greatest interest in the benevolent enterprise.
From some letters given in the *Memoirs of Mrs.
Fry* it seems that the Empress felt a true womanly compassion for the inmates of the Government Lunatic Asylum, and inaugurated a system
of more rational treatment. How far her influence on behalf of the imprisoned and insane
was induced and fostered by the English Quakeress, was never fully known until after her
death, when a most interesting letter, addressed
to the children of Mrs. Fry, was published.
This letter was sent to them by Mr. John
Venning, brother to Walter Venning, who had
opened the correspondence, but who had, like
the benevolent lady with whom it was maintained, "passed over to the majority." From
this correspondence it was found that the
Emperor and Empress of Russia, the Princess
Sophia Mestchersky, Prince Galitzin, and many
ladies of high rank, had been stirred up to

befriend those who had fallen under the strong
arm of the law, and to make their captivity
more productive, if possible, of good results.
Not only so, but lunatics, more helpless than
prisoners, had been cared for, as the outcome of
Mrs. Fry's visits to St. Petersburg, and her
communications with the powers that were at
that era. With these preliminary words of
explanation, the subjoined letter speaks for
itself : —

I cheerfully comply with your desire to be furnished
with some of the most striking and useful points contained in your late beloved mother's correspondence
with myself in Russia, relative to the improvement of
the Lunatic Asylum in St. Petersburg. I the more
readily engage in this duty, because I am persuaded
that its publication may, under the Lord's blessing,
prove of great service to many such institutions on
the Continent, as well as in Great Britain. . . . I begin
by stating that her correspondence was invaluable, as
regarded the treatment and management of both prisoners and insane people. It was the fruit of her own
rich practical experience communicated with touching
simplicity, and it produced lasting benefits to these institutions in Russia. In 1827, I informed your dear mother
that I had presented to the Emperor Nicholas a statement of the defects of the Government Lunatic Asylum,
which could only be compared to our own old Bedlam in
London, fifty years since; and that the dowager Empress
had sent for me to the Winter Palace, when she most
kindly, and I may say, joyfully, informed me that she and
her august son, the Emperor, had visited together this

abode of misery. They were convinced of the necessity, not only of having a new building, but also of
a complete reform in the management of the insane;
and further that the Emperor had requested her to
take it under her own care, and to appoint me the
governor of it. I must observe that in the meantime
the old asylum was immediately improved, as much
as the building allowed, for the introduction of your
dear mother's admirable system. Shortly after, I had
the pleasure of accompanying the Empress to examine a
palace-like house — Prince Sherbatoff's — having above
two miles of garden, and a fine stream of water running
through the grounds, situated only five miles from St.
Petersburg. The next day an order was given to purchase
it. I was permitted to send the plan of this immense
building to your dear mother for her inspection, as
well as to ask from her hints for its improvement.
Two extensive wings were recommended, and subsequently added for dormitories. The wings cost about
£15,000, and in addition to this sum from the Government, the Emperor, who was always ready to promote
the cause of benevolence, gave three thousand pounds
for cast-iron window-frames, recommended by your dear
mother, as the clumsy iron bars which had been used
in the old institution had induced many a poor inmate,
when looking at them, to say with a sigh, " Sir, prison,
prison ! " Your dear mother also strongly recommended
that all, except the violent lunatics, should dine together
at a table covered with a cloth, and furnished with plates
and spoons.

The former method of serving out the food was most
disgusting. This new plan delighted the Empress, and
I soon received an order to meet her at the asylum. On
her arrival she requested that a table should be covered,

and then desired me to go round and invite the inmates to come and dine. Sixteen came immediately, and sat down. The Empress approached the table, and ordered one of the upper servants to sit at the head of it and to ask a blessing. When the servant arose to do this, they all stood up. The soup, with small pieces of meat, was then regularly served; and as soon as dinner was finished, they all rose up spontaneously and thanked the Empress for her motherly kindness. I saw that the kind Empress was deeply moved, and turning to me she said, "*Mon Cher*, this is one of the happiest days of my life." The next day the number increased at table, and so it continued increasing. After your dear mother's return from Ireland, where she had been visiting, among other institutions, the lunatic asylums, she wrote me a letter on the great importance of supplying the lunatics with the Scriptures. This letter deserved to be written in letters of gold; I sent it to the Imperial family; it excited the most pleasing feelings and marked approbation. The court physician, His Excellency Dr. Riehl, a most enlightened and devoted philanthropist, came to me for a copy of it. It removed all the difficulty there had been respecting giving the Holy Scriptures to the inmates. I was therefore permitted to furnish them with copies, in their various languages. It may be useful to state the result of this measure, which was considered by some to be a wild and dangerous proceeding. I soon found groups collected together, listening patiently and quietly to one of their number reading the New Testament. Instead of disturbing their minds, it soothed and delighted them. I have witnessed a poor lunatic, a Frenchman, during an interval of returning reason, reading the New Testament in his bed-room, with tears running down his cheeks ; also a Russian priest, a lunatic, collect a number together, while he read to them the Word of God.

On one occasion I witnessed a most interesting scene. On entering the institution, I found a young woman dying; her eyes were closed, and she was apparently breathing her last breath. I ordered one of the servants of the institution to read very loud to her that verse, " For God so loved the world, that He gave His only begotten Son, that whosoever believeth on Him should not perish, but have everlasting life." Dr. K—— observed, " Sir, she is almost dead, and it is useless." On my urging its being done, lo! to the astonishment of all present, she opened her eyes and smiled. I said: " Is it sweet, my dear?", She nodded assent. " Shall it be read to you again?" A smile and nod of the head followed. She evidently possessed her reason at that moment, and who can trace, or limit, the operation of the Holy Spirit, on the reading of God's' own Word even in her circumstances?

When I received a letter from your mother I always wrote it out in French, and presented it in that language to the Empress; and when she had read it, it was very encouraging to see with what alacrity she ordered one of her secretaries to translate it into Russian, and then deliver it to me to be conveyed to the asylum, and entered into the journal there, for immediate adoption. I remember on one occasion, taking a list of rules, at least fourteen in number, and the same day were confirmed by the Empress. These rules introduced the following important arrangements; viz., the treating the inmates, as far as possible as sane persons, both in conversation and manners toward them; to allow them as much liberty as possible; to engage them daily to take exercise in the open air; to allow them to wear their own clothes and no uniform prison-dress; also to break up the inhuman system of permitting the promiscuous idle curiosity of the public, so that no one was allowed to see them without permission; a room, on entering the asylum, was prepared for one at a time, on certain days, to see their relations. The old cruel system drew forth many angry expressions from the poor lunatics : " Are we, then, wild beasts, to be gazed at ? "

The Empress made a present to the institution of a piano-forte; it had also a hand-organ, which pleased the poor inmates exceedingly. On one occasion the Empress, on entering the asylum, observed that the inmates appeared unusually dull, when she called them near, and played on the hand-organ herself an enlivening tune.

Another important rule of your mother's was, most strictly to fulfill whatever you promise to any of the inmates, and, above all, to exercise patience, gentleness, kindness, and love towards them; therefore, to be exceedingly careful as to the character of the keepers you appoint. These are some of the pleasing results of your mother's work. The dowager Empress, on one occasion, conversing about your mother, said : " How much I should like to see that excellent woman, Madame Fry, in Russia; " and often did I indulge that wish. What a meeting it would have been, between two such devoted philanthropists as your mother and the dowager Empress, who was daily devoting her time and fortune to doing good. . . . Although the Empress was in her sixty-ninth year, I had the felicity of accompanying her in no less than eleven of her personal visits to the Lunatic Asylum, say from February to October, 1828. On the 24th of October she died, to the deep-felt regret of the whole empire. Rozoff, a young lunatic, as soon as he heard it, burst into tears. She would visit each lunatic, when bodily afflicted, and send an easy chair for one, and nicely-dressed meat for others; and weekly send from the palace wine, coffee, tea, sugar and fruit for their use.

Among the many striking features in your mother's correspondence, her love to the Word of God, and her desire for its general circulation, were very apparent. Evidently, that sacred book was the fountain whence she herself derived all that strength and grace to carry on her work of faith and labor of love, which her Divine Master so richly blessed. . . . In December 1827, when accompanying the Emperor Nicholas through the new Litoffsky Prison, he was not only well pleased to find every cell fully supplied with the Scriptures — the rich result of his having confirmed the late Emperor Alexander's orders to give the Scriptures gratis to all the prisoners — but on seeing some Jews in the prison he said to me : " I hope you also furnish these poor people with them, that they may become Christians; I pity them." I witnessed a most touching scene on the Emperor's entering the debtors' room; three old, venerable, gray-headed men fell on their knees and cried, " Father, have mercy on us ! " The Emperor stretched out his hand in the peculiar grandeur of his manner, and said : " Rise; all your debts are paid; from this moment you are free "; without knowing the amount of the debts, one of which was very considerable. I hope this feeble attempt to detail a little of your dear mother's useful work may be acceptable, leaving you to make what use of it you think proper.

Such testimonies as these must have been peculiarly grateful to Mrs. Fry's family, be- cause it is natural to desire not only success in any good work, but also grateful remembrance and appreciation of it. Sometimes, however, the reverse was the case ; even those whom she had endeavored to serve had turned out ungrateful, impudent and hardened. Yet her loving pity followed even them : still, like the Lord whom she served, she loved them in spite of their repulsiveness and ingratitude. And when some notably ungrateful things were reported to her respecting the female convicts on board the *Amphitrite*, she only prayed and sorrowed for them the more. Especially was this the case when she heard that the ship had gone down on the French coast, bearing to their tomb beneath the sad sea waves, the 120 women, with their children, being conveyed in her to New South Wales. Not one hard thought did she entertain of them : all was charity, sorrow and tenderness. And if for one little moment her new theories as to the treatment of criminals seemed to be broken down, never for an instant did she set them aside. She knew that perfection could only be attained after many long years of trial and probation. While undermining the old ideas, she set herself an equally gigantic task in establishing the new.

CHAPTER XII.

HITHERTO our little monograph has dealt mainly with Mrs. Fry's *public* life and work. Possibly, however, the reader may now feel curious to know how she bore the strain of private responsibilities; how as a wife, mother, neighbor, and Christian, she performed the duties which usually fall to people in those positions. It does not appear that she was wanting in any of them.

As the wife of a city merchant, as the mistress, until reverses came, of a large household, as the mother of a numerous family of boys and girls, and as the plain Friend, and minister among Friends, she seems to have fulfilled the duties which devolved upon her with quiet, cheerful simplicity, persevering conscientiousness, and prayerful earnestness. She was much the same in sunshine and in shadow, in losses and in prosperity; her only anxiety was to do what was right. From the revelations of her journal we find that self-examination caused her frequently to put into the form of writing, the questions which harassed her soul. There can be no reasonable doubt that she *was* harassed as all over-conscientious people are — with the fear and consciousness that her duties were not half done. How few of this class ever contemplate themselves or their works with anything like satisfaction! A short extract from her journal penned during the first years of her wedded life affords the key to this self-examination, a self-examination which was strictly continued as long as reason held her sway. This entry is entitled "Questions for Myself."

"First. — Hast thou this day been honest and true in performing thy duty towards thy Creator in the first place, and secondly towards thy fellow-creatures ; or hast thou sophisticated and flinched ?

"Second. — Hast thou been vigilant in frequently pausing, in the hurry and career of the day, to see who thou art endeavoring to serve : whether thy Maker or thyself? And every time that trial or temptation assailed thee, didst thou endeavor to look steadily at the Delivering Power, even to Christ who can do all things for thee ?

"Third. — Hast thou endeavored to perform thy relative duties faithfully ; been a tender, loving, yielding wife, where thy own will and pleasure were concerned, a tender yet steady mother with thy children, making thyself quickly and strictly obeyed, but careful in what thou requirest of them; a kind yet honest mistress, telling thy servants their faults, when thou thinkest it for their or thy good, but never unnecessarily worrying thyself or them about trifles, and to everyone endeavoring to do as thou wouldst be done unto?"

A life governed by these principles, and measured by these rules, was not likely to be otherwise than strictly, severely, nervously good. We use the word "nervously" because here and there, up and down the pages of her journal are scattered numerous passages full of such questions as the above. None ever peered into their hearts, or searched their lives more relentlessly than she did. Upright, self-denying, just, pure, charitable, "hoping all things, bearing all things, believing all things," she judged herself by a stricter law than she judged others; condemning in herself what she allowed to be expedient, if not lawful, in others, and laying bare her inmost heart before her God. After she had done all that she judged it to be her duty to do, she humbly and tearfully acknowledged herself to be one of the Lord's most "unprofitable servants." It would be useless to endeavor to measure such a life by any rules of worldly polity or fashions. An extract written at this time, relative to the welfare and treatment of servants, may be of use in showing how she permitted her sound sense and practical daily piety to decide for her in emergencies and anxieties growing out of the "mistress and servant" question. "At this time there is no set of people I feel so much about as servants ; as I do not think they have generally justice done to them. They are too much considered as another race of beings, and we are apt to forget that the holy injunction holds good with them : 'As ye would that men should do to you, do ye even so to them.' I believe in striving to do so we shall not take them out of their station in life, but endeavor to render them happy and contented in it, and be truly their friends, though not their familiars or equals, as to the things of this life. We have reason to believe that the difference in our stations is ordered by a wiser than ourselves, who directs us how to fill our different places ; but we must endeavor never to forget that in the best sense we are all one, and, though our paths may be different, we have all souls equally valuable, and have all the same work to do, which, if properly considered, should lead us to have great sympathy and love, and also a constant care for their welfare, both here and hereafter. We greatly misunderstand each

other (I mean servants and masters in general) ;
I fully believe, partly from our different situations in life, and partly from our different edu-
cations, and the way in which each party is apt
to view the other. Masters and mistresses are
greatly deficient, I think, in a general way ; and
so are most servants towards them ; it is for
both to keep in view strictly to do unto others
as they would be done unto, and also to remember that we are indeed all one with God."

As the mother of a large family, Mrs. Fry
endeavored to do her duty faithfully and lovingly. Twelve sons and daughters were given to
her, trained by her more or less, with reference
not only to their temporal welfare, but their
spiritual also. In all the years of motherhood
many cares attached themselves to her. Illness,
the deaths of near relatives, and of one little
child, the marriage of some of her children out
of the Society of Friends, losses in business,
and consequent reduction of household comforts
and pleasures, the censure which sometimes followed her most disinterested acts, and the
exaggerated praise of others, all combined to
try her character and her spirit. Through it all
she moved and lived, like one who was surrounded with an angelic company of witnesses ;
desirous only of laying up such a life-record that
she could with calmness face it in "that day for
which all other days are made."

One after another the little fledglings came to the home-nest, to be cared for, trained up, and fitted for their peculiar niches in life. But in 1815, a new sorrow came to the fireside; the angel reaper Death cut down the little Eliza-beth, the seventh child, nearly five years of age, and the special darling of the band. Her illness was very short, scarcely lasting a week; but even during that illness her docile, intelligent spirit exhibited itself in new and more endear-ing phases. Death was only anticipated during the last few hours of life, and when the fatal issue appeared but too certain the parents sat in agonized silence, watching the darling whom they could not save. Mrs. Fry begged earnestly of the Great Disposer of life and death that he would spare the child, if consonant with His holy will; but when the end came, and the child had passed "through the pearly gates into the city" she uttered an audible thanksgiving that she was at last where neither sin, sorrow, nor death could have any dominion. No words can do justice to this event like her own, writ-ten in her journal at that time. The pages recall all a mother's love and yearning tender-ness, together with a Christian's strong confi-dence: —

It has pleased Almighty and Infinite Wisdom to take from us our most dear and tenderly-beloved child little

Betsy, between four and five years old. In receiving her, as well as giving her back again, we have, I believe, been enabled to bless the Sacred Name. She was a very precious child, of much wisdom for her years, and, I can hardly help believing, much grace; liable to the frailty of childhood, at times she would differ with the little ones and rather loved her own way, but she was very easy to lead though not one to be driven. She had most tender affections, a good understanding for her years, and a remarkably staid and solid mind. Her love was very strong, and her little attentions great to those she loved, and remarkable in her kindness to servants, poor people, and all animals; she had much feeling for them; but what was more, the bent of her mind was remarkably toward serious things. It was a subject she loved to dwell upon: she would often talk of "Almighty God," and almost everything that had connection with Him. On Third Day, after some suffering of body from great sickness, she appeared wonderfully relieved . . . and began by telling me how many hymns and stories she knew, with her countenance greatly animated, a flush on her cheeks, her eyes very bright, and a smile of inexpressible content, almost joy. I think she first said, with a powerful voice, —

> How glorious is our Heavenly King,
> Who reigns above the sky;

and then expressed how beautiful it was, and how the little children that die stand before Him; but she did not remember all the words of the hymn, nor could I help her. She then mentioned other hymns, and many sweet things . . . her heart appeared inexpressibly to overflow with love. Afterwards she told me one or two droll stories, and made clear and bright comments as she went along; then stopped a little while, and said in the

fullness of her heart, and the joy of a little innocent
child . . . " Mamma, I love everybody better than myself, and I love thee better than anybody, and I love
Almighty much better than thee, and I hope thee loves
Almighty much better than me." . . . I appeared to satisfy her that it was so. This was on Third Day morning,
and she was a corpse on Fifth Day evening; but in her
death there was abundant cause for thanksgiving; prayer
appeared indeed to be answered, as very little if any suffering seemed to attend her, and no struggle at last, but
her breathing grew more and more slow and gentle, till
she ceased to breathe at all. During the day, being
from time to time strengthened in prayer, in heart, and
in word, I found myself only led to ask for her that she
might be for ever with her God, whether she remained
much longer in time or not; but, that if it pleased Infinite Wisdom her sufferings might be mitigated, and as
far as it was needful for her to suffer that she might be
sustained. This was marvellously answered beyond anything we could expect from the nature of the complaint.
. . . I desire never to forget this favor, but, if it please
Infinite Wisdom, to be preserved from repining or unduly
giving way to lamentation for losing so sweet a child.
. . . I have been permitted to feel inexpressible pangs at
her loss, though at first it was so much like partaking
with her in joy and glory, that I could not mourn if. I
would, only rejoice almost with joy unspeakable and full
of glory. But if a very deep baptism was afterwards permitted me, like the enemy coming in as a flood ; but even
here a way for escape has been made, my supplication
answered . . . and the bitter cup sweetened; but at
others my loss has touched me in a manner almost inexpressible, to awake and find my much-loved little girl so
totally fled from my view, so many pleasant pictures

marred. As far as I am concerned, I view it as a separation from a sweet source of comfort and enjoyment,
but surely not a real evil. Abundant comforts are left
me if it please my kind and Heavenly Father to provide
me power to enjoy them, and continually in heart to
return him thanks for His unutterable loving kindness to
my tenderly-beloved little one, who had so sweet and
easy a life and so tranquil a death. . . . My much-loved
husband and I have drunk this cup together in close
sympathy and unity of feeling. It has at times been
very bitter to us both; but as an outward alleviation, we
have, I believe, been in measure each other's joy and
helpers. The sweet children have also tenderly sympa-
thized; brothers, sisters, servants, and friends, have
been very near and dear in showing their kindness not
only to the darling child, but to me, and to us all. . . .
We find outwardly and inwardly, "the Lord did provide."

The little lost Betsey, who "just came to show
how sweet a flower for Paradise could bloom,"
was thenceforth a sacred memory ; for from that
day they had a connecting link between their
household and the skies. Very frequently, even
in the midst of her multifarious engagements,
her thoughts wandered off to the little grave
in Barking burying-ground, where rested the
remains of the dear child, and, perchance, a ten-
derer tone crept into her voice as she dealt with
the outcast children of prisons and reformatories.
Soon after this event the elder boys and girls
went to school among their relatives, and only

the youngest were left at Plashet House with her. As a new baby came within six months after little Betsey's death, the motherly hands were still full. She found, however, time to write letters of wise and mother-like counsels.

My much-loved girls:— Your letters received last evening gave us much pleasure. I anxiously hope that you will now do your utmost in whatever respects your education, not only on your own account, but for our sake. I look forward to your return with so much comfort, as useful and valuable helpers to me, which you will be all the more if you get forward yourselves. I see quite a field of useful service and enjoyment for you, should we be favored to meet under comfortable circumstances in the spring. I mean that you should have a certain department to fill in the house, amongst the children and the poor, as well as your own studies and enjoyments; I think there was not often a brighter opening for two girls. Plashet is, after all, such a home, it now looks sweetly; and your little room is almost a temptation to me to take it for a sitting-room for myself, it is so pretty and so snug; it is newly furnished, and looks very pleasant indeed. The poor, and the school, will, I think, be glad to have you home, for help is wanted in these things. Indeed, if your hearts are but turned the right way, you may, I believe, be made instruments of much good, and I shall be glad to have the day come that I may introduce you into prisons and hospitals. . . . This appears to me to be your present business — to give all diligence to your present duties; and I cannot help believing, if this be the case, that the day will come when you will be brought into much usefulness.

As the years rolled on, her boys went to school also ; but they were followed by a loving mother's counsels. From her correspondence with them we cull a few extracts to prove how constant and tender was her care over them, and how far-reaching her anxieties. Two or three specimens will suffice.

Upon the departure of each of her boys for boarding-school she wrote out and gave him a copy of the following rules. They are valuable, as showing how carefully she watched over their mental and moral welfare.

" 1st. Be regular, strict in attending to religious duties ; and do not allow other boys around thee to prevent thy having some portion of time for reading at least a text of Scripture, meditation and prayer ; and if it appear to be a duty, flinch not from bowing the knee before them, as a mark of thy allegiance to the King of Kings and Lord of Lords. Attend diligently when the holy Scriptures are read, or to any other religious instruction, and endeavor in Meeting to seek after a serious waiting state of mind, and to watch unto prayer. Let First Day be well employed in reading proper books, etc., but also enjoy the rest of innocent recreation, afforded in admiring the beauties of nature ; for I believe this is right in the ordering of a kind Providence that there should be some rest and recreation in it. Show a proper, bold, and manly spirit in maintaining among thy play-fellows a religious character, and strict attention to all religious duties. Remember these texts to strengthen thee in it. 'For whosoever shall be ashamed of Me, and My words, of him shall the Son of Man be ashamed, when He shall come in His own glory, in His Father's, and of the holy angels.' 'But I say unto you, whosoever shall confess Me before men, him shall the Son of Man also confess before the angels of God ; but he that denieth Me before man shall be denied before the angels of God.' Now, the sooner the dread laugh of the world loses its power, the better for you. . . But strongly as I advise thee thus faithfully maintaining thy principles and doing thy duty, I would have thee very careful of either judging or reproving others ; for it takes a long time to get the beam out of our own eye, before we can see clearly to take the mote out of our brother's eye. There is for one young in years, much greater safety in preaching to others by example, than in word, or doing what is done in an upright, manly spirit, 'unto the Lord, and not unto man.'

" 2d. I shall not speak of moral conduct, which, if religious principles be kept to, we may believe will be good ; but I shall give cer-

tain hints that may point out the temptations
to which schools are particularly liable. I have
observed a want of strict integrity in school-
boys, as it respects their schoolmasters and
teachers — a disposition to cheat them, to do
that behind their backs which they would not
do before their faces, and so having two faces.
Now, this is a subject of the utmost importance
— to maintain truth and integrity upon all
points. Be not double-minded in any degree,
but faithfully maintain, not only the upright
principle on religious ground, but also the
brightest honor, according to the maxims of the
world. I mourn to say I have seen the want of
this bright honor, not only in school-boys, but
in some of our highly-professing society ; and
my belief is that it cannot be too strictly maintained, or too early begun. I like to see it in
small things, and in great; for it marks the
upright man. I may say that I abhor anything
like being under-handed or double-dealing; but
let us go on the right and noble principle of
doing to others as we would have others do to
us ; therefore, in all transactions, small and
great, maintain strictly the correct, upright, and
most honorable practice. I have heard of boys
robbing their neighbors' fruit, etc. ; I may truly
say that I believe there are very few in the
present day would do such things, but no cir-

cumstances can make this other than a shameful deviation from all honest and right principles. My belief is, that such habits begun in
youth end mostly in great incorrectness in future life, if not in gross sin ; and that no excuse
can be pleaded for such actions, for sin is
equally sin, whether committed by the school-
boy or those of mature years, which is too apt
to be forgotten, and that punishment *will* follow."

In a letter to her eldest son she begs him to
try to be a learned man, not to neglect the modern languages ; but so to improve his time at
school that he may become in manhood a power
for good ; and then, by various thoughtful kindnesses manifests her unwearying care for his
welfare.

She gratefully acknowledges, in another communication to a sister, the assistance which that
sister rendered in educating some of the elder
girls, for a time, so enabling Mrs. Fry herself
to be set free for the multitude of other duties
awaiting her.

As years rolled by, an acute cause of sorrow
to her was the marriage of one, then another of
her numerous family out of the Society. They
mostly married into families connected with the
Church of England ; but as the Society of
Friends disunite from membership all who

marry out of it, and as parents are blamed for permitting such unions, her sorrow was somewhat heavy. She even anticipated being cut off from the privilege of ministry in the Society; but to the credit of that Society, it does not appear that it silenced her in return for the forsaking, by her children, of "the old paths." Whether Quakerism was too old-fashioned and strict for the young people, or the attractions of families other than Friends more powerful, we cannot say. However, it seems that the young folks grew up to be useful and God-fearing in the main, so that the Church universal lost nothing by their transference into other communions.

> When joy seems highest
> Then sorrow is nighest,

says the old rhyme. An experience of this sort came to Mrs. Fry. One of her children had just married an estimable member of the Society of Friends, and while rejoicing with the young couple, she appeared to be drawn out in thankfulness for the many mercies vouchsafed to her. Her cup seemed brimming over with joy; and after the bridal party had departed, one of her daughters came across the lawn to remark to her mother on the beauty of the scene, finishing by a reference to the temporal prosperity which was granted them. Mrs. Fry could do no other than acquiesce in the sentiments expressed, but added, with almost prophetic insight, "But I have remarked that when great outward prosperity is granted it is often permitted to precede great trials." This was in the summer of 1828 ; before that year ended the family was struggling in the waves of adversity, losses, and trials — struggling, indeed, to preserve that honest name which had hitherto been the pride of Mr. Fry's firm.

One of the houses of business with which Mr. Fry was connected at this time failed, and his income was largely diminished. The house which he personally conducted was still able to meet all its obligations ; but the blow in connection with this other firm was so staggering that they were forced to submit to the pressure of straitened means, at least for a time. We are told, indeed, by Mrs. Fry's daughters, that this failure "involved Mrs. Fry and her family in a train of sorrows and perplexities which tinged the remaining years of her life." The strict principles and the not less strict discipline of the Society of Friends rendered her course of action at that juncture very doubtful. Occupying the prominent positions she had before the nation — indeed before the world, for Mrs. Fry's name was a household word —it seemed impossible to her upright spirit to face the usual

Meeting on First Day. Her sensitive spirit winced acutely at the reproach which *might perchance* be cast upon the name of religion; but after a prayerful pause she and her husband went, accompanied by their children — at least such of them as were then at home. She occupied her usual place at the Meeting, but the big tears rolling down her face in quick succession, testified to the sorrow and anguish which then became her lot. Yet before the session ended she rose, calmed herself, and spoke, most thrillingly, from the words, "Though He slay me, yet will I trust in Him," while the listeners manifested their sympathy by tears and words of sorrow. In November of that sad year she wrote the following letter to one of her children, in reference to the trial : —

I do not like to pour out my sorrows too heavily upon thee, nor do I like to keep thee in the dark as to our real state. This is, I consider, one of the deepest trials to which we are liable; its perplexities are so great and numerous, its mortifications and humiliations so abounding, and its sorrows so deep. None can tell, but those who have passed through it, the anguish of heart at times felt; but, thanks be to God, this extreme state of distress has not been very frequent, nor its continuance very long. I frequently find my mind in degree sheathed against the deep sorrows, and am enabled not to look so much at them; but there are also times when secondary things arise, such as parting with servants, schools, the

poor around us, and our dear home. These things over-
whelm me ; indeed, I think naturally I have a very acute
sense of the sorrow. Then the bright side of the picture
arises. I have found such help and strength in prayer
to God, and highly mysterious as this dispensation may
be in some points of view, yet I think I have frequently,
if not generally, been able to say, " Not as I will, but as
Thou wilt," and bow under it. All our children and chil-
dren-in-law, my brothers and sisters, our many friends
and servants, have been a strong consolation to me.

It was not possible, however, for Mrs. Fry to
suffer without experiencing an unwonted measure of sympathy from all classes of the community. Many hearts followed her most lovingly
in these hours of humiliation and sorrow ; and
when it was known that she must leave Plashet
House, the tide of deep sympathy overflowed
more than one heart. As a preliminary step
the family moved, first to St. Mildred's Court,
then to the home of their eldest son. The business which had been carried on there by Mr.
Fry and his father was now conducted by his
sons ; and by this the young men were enabled
to provide for the comfort of their parents.
Their bidding good-bye to Plashet, however,
entailed very much that was sad to others.
The schools hitherto supported by the Frys
were handed over to the care of the vicar of the
parish ; many old pensioners and servants had
to be given over to the kindness of others, or in

some cases, possibly, to the not very tender mercies of "the parish;" while she herself, who had always laid it down as an indispensable rule to be *just* before being generous, was com-pelled to conform her manner of life to some-what narrow means.

Shakespeare says: "Sorrow comes not in sin-gle spies but in battalions," and experience proves the adage to be true. William Fry, the eldest son of the family, was thrown upon a bed of illness, as the result of an over-strained and exhausted brain; soon after, sickness spread through the whole family, until the house, and even Plashet, — which, being empty, afforded them a temporary shelter, — became a hospital on a small scale. Yet at this time the kindly letters of sympathy and condolence received from all quarters must have comforted and cheered her anguished spirit. From a number of such communications we give two, one from William Wilberforce, the other from Mrs. Opie. Wilberforce wrote : —

You, I doubt not, will be enabled to *feel*, as well as to know, that even this event will be one of those which, in your instance, are working for good. You have been enabled to exhibit a bright specimen of Christian excel-lence in *doing* the will of God, and, I doubt not, you will manifest a similar specimen in the harder and more diffi-cult exercise of *suffering* it. I have often thought that we are sometimes apt to forget that key, for unlocking what we deem to be very mysterious dispensations of Providence, in the misfortunes and afflictions of eminent servants of God, that is afforded by a passage in St. Paul's Epistle to his beloved Phillipians : " Unto you it is given, not only to believe on Him, but also to suffer for His sake." It is the strong only that will be selected for exhibiting these graces which require peculiar strength. May you, my dear friend (indeed, I doubt not you will), be enabled to bear the whole will of God with cheerful confidence in His unerring wisdom and unfailing goodness. May every loss of this world's wealth be more than compensated by a larger measure of the unsearchable riches of Christ. . . . Meanwhile you are richly provided with relatives and friends whom you love so well as to relish receiving kindnesses from them, as well as the far easier office of doing them. . . .

In reply to this, it would seem that Mrs. Fry, while thankful for the sympathy manifested on all hands, doubted the advisability of resuming her benevolent labors among prisons and hospitals. Mr. Wilberforce proved himself again a wise and far-seeing counsellor. He wrote : —

I cannot delay assuring you that I do not see how it is possible for any reasonable being to doubt the propriety . . . or, rather, let me say *the absolute duty* — of your renewing your prison visitations. A gracious Providence has blessed you with success in your endeavors to impress a set of miserables, whose character and circumstances might almost have extinguished hope ; and you will return to them, if with diminished pecuniary powers, yet, we may trust, through the mercy and goodness of our Heavenly Father, with powers of a far higher order unimpaired, and with the augmented respect and regard of every sound judgment . . . for having borne with becoming disposition a far harder trial certainly than any stroke which proceeds immediately from the hand of God. May you continue, my dear Madam, to be the honored instrument of great and rare benefits to almost the most pitiable of your fellow-creatures.

The *Record* newspaper had suggested that additional contributions should be sent to the chief of the societies which had been inaugurated by Mrs. Fry, and so largely supported by her. The Marquis of Cholmondeley wrote to Mrs. Opie, inquiring of that lady fuller particulars of the disaster, in so far as it affected or was likely to affect Mrs. Fry's benevolent work. He had been a staunch friend of her labors, having seconded them many times when the life of a wretched felon was at stake ; and now, continuing the interest which he had hitherto exhibited, he was fearful lest this business calamity would put a stop to many of those labors. Mrs. Opie, whose friendship dated from the old Norwich days, lost no time in writing as follows to her suffering friend : —

Though I have not hitherto felt free in mind to write to thee, my very dear friend, under thy present most severe trial, thou hast been continually, I may say, in my thoughts, brought feelingly and solemnly before me, both day and night. I must also tell thee that, two nights ago,

I had a pleasing, cheering dream of thee : — I saw thee looking thy best, dressed with peculiar care and neatness, and smiling so brightly that I could not help stroking thy cheek, and saying, " Dear friend ! it is quite delightful to me to see thee looking thus again, so like the Betsey Fry of former days : " and then I woke. But this sweet image of thee lives with me still. . . . Since your trials were known, I have rarely, if ever, opened a page of Scripture without finding some promise applicable to thee and thine. I do not believe that I was looking for them, but they presented themselves unsought, and gave me comfort and confidence. Do not suppose, dear friend, that I am not fully aware of the peculiar bitterness and suffering which attends this trial in thy situation to thy own individual feeling ; but, then, how precious and how cheering to thee must be the evidence it has called forth, of the love and respect of those who are near and dear to thee, and of the public at large. Adversity is indeed the time to try the hearts of our friends ; and it must be now, or will be in future, a cordial to thee to remember that thou hast proved how truly and generally thou art beloved and reverenced.

Mrs. Fry's health failed very much during the dreary months which followed. Nor was this all, for trials, mental and spiritual, seemed to crowd around her. It was indeed, though on a scale fitted to her capacity, "the hour and power of darkness." She says in her journal, that her soul was bowed down within her, and her eyes were red with weeping. Yet she rallied again. After spending some months with their eldest son, William, at Mildred's Court,

Mr. and Mrs. Fry removed to a small but convenient villa in Upton Lane, nearly adjoining the house and grounds of her brother, Samuel Gurney. This house was not only to be a place of refuge in the dark and cloudy days of calamity, but to become, in its turn, famous for the visits of princes and nobles, who thus sought to do honor to her who dwelt in it. Writing in her journal, on June 10th, 1829, Mrs. Fry said : —

We are now nearly settled in this, our new abode ; and I may say, although the house and garden are small, yet it is pleasant and convenient and I am fully satisfied, and, I hope, thankful for such a home. I have at times been favored to feel great peace, and I may say joy in the Lord — a sort of seal to the important step taken ; though at others the extreme disorder into which our things have been brought by all these changes, the pain of leaving Plashet, the difficulty of making new arrangements, has harassed and tried me. But I trust it will please a kind Providence to bless my endeavor to have and to keep my house in order. Place is a matter of small importance, if that peace which the world cannot give be our portion. . . . Although a large garden is now my allotment, I feel pleasure in having even a small one; and my acute relish for the beautiful in nature and art is on a clear day almost constantly gratified by a view of Greenwich Hospital and Park, and other parts of Kent; the shipping on the river, as well as the cattle feeding in the meadows. So that in small things as well as great, spiritual and temporal, I have yet reason to . . . bless and magnify the name of my Lord.

Two of her nieces accompanied her, in 1834, upon a mission to the Friends' Meetings in Dorset and Hants ; and recalling this journey some time later, one of them said, speaking of her aunt's peculiar mission of ministering to the tried and afflicted : " There was no weakness or trouble of mind or body, which might not safely be unveiled to her. Whatever various or opposite views, feelings, or wishes might be confided to her, all came out again tinged with her own loving, hopeful spirit. Bitterness of every kind died when entrusted to her ; it never re-appeared. The most favorable construction possible was always put upon every transaction. No doubt her feeling lay this way ; but did it not give her and her example a wonderful influence ? Was it not the very secret of her power with the wretched and degraded prisoners ? She could always see hope for everyone ; she invariably found or made some point of light. The most abandoned must have felt she did not despair for them, either for this world or for another ; and this it was which made her irresistible."

In taking a view of this good woman's religious life and character, it will be helpful to see her as she appeared to herself — to enter into her own feelings at different periods of her life, and to listen to her heart-felt expressions of

humility and perplexity. Thus, in relation to
the ups and downs of life with her, we find in
her journal this passage : —

The difference between last winter and this winter
has been striking! How did the righteous compass me
about, from the Sovereign, the Princes, and the Princesses, down to the poorest, lowest, and most destitute;
how did poor sinners of almost every description seek
after me, and cleave to me ? What was not said of me ?
What was not thought of me, may I not say, in public
and in private, in innumerable publications ? This winter
I have had the bed of languishing; deep, very deep,
prostration of soul and body ; instead of being a helper
to others, ready to lean upon all, glad even to be diverted
by a child's book. In addition to this, I find the tongue
of slander has been ready to attack me. The work that
was made so much of before, some try to lessen now.
My faith is that He will not give me over to the will of
my enemies, nor let me be utterly cast down.

In relation to her conscientious fear of the
admixture of sin with her service of God and of
humanity, she wrote : —

I apprehend that all would not understand me, but
many who are much engaged in what we call works of
righteousness, will understand the reason that in the
Jewish dispensation there was an offering made for the
iniquity of *holy things*.

In regard to marriage she writes : —

We have had the subject of marriage much before us
this year ; it has brought us to some test of our feelings

and principles respecting it. That it is highly desirable to have young persons settle in marriage, I cannot doubt, and that it is one of the most likely means of their preservation, religiously, morally, temporally. More-over, it is highly desirable to settle with one of the same religious views, habits, and education, as themselves, more particularly for those who have been brought up as Friends, because their mode of education is peculiar. But if any young persons, upon arriving at an age of dis-cretion, do not feel themselves really attached to our peculiar views and habits, then, I think, their parents have no right to use undue influence with them as to the connections they may incline to form, provided they be with persons of religious lives and conversation. I am of opinion that parents are apt to exercise too much authority upon the subject of marriage, and that there would be really more happy unions if young persons were left more to their own feelings and discretion. Marriage is too much treated like a business concern, and love, that essential ingredient, too little respected in it. I disapprove of the rule of our Society which disowns persons for allowing a child to marry one who is not a Friend; it is a most undue and unchristian restraint, as far as I can judge of it.

As the time passed, and her family got scat-tered up and down in the world, the idea occurred to her that, although members of dif-ferent sects and churches, they could unite in fireside worship and study of the Bible, *as Christians.* Many of them were within suitable distances for occasional or frequent meetings, according to their circumstances ; while some

of the grandchildren were of an age to understand, and possibly profit by, the exercises. In
response to the motherly communication which
follows, these family gatherings were arranged,
and succeeded beyond the original expectations
of her who suggested them. They continued,
under the title of "philanthropic evenings," to
cement the family circle, after Mrs. Fry had
passed away. The tone of the letter inviting
their co-operation is that of a philanthropist, a
mother, and a Christian. It shows plainly that
with all her engagements, worries and trials,
she had not absorbed or lost the spirit of the
docile Mary in that of the careful Martha.

My Dearest Children:

Many of you know that for some time I have
felt and expressed the want of our social intercourse
at times, leading to religious union and communion
among us. It has pleased the Almighty to permit that
by far the larger number of you no longer walk with
me in my religious course. Except very occasionally,
we do not meet together for the solemn purpose of worship, and upon some other points we do not see eye to
eye; and whilst I feel deeply sensible that, notwithstanding this diversity among us, we are truly united in our
Holy Head, there are times when, in my declining years,
I seriously feel the loss of not having more of the spiritual help and encouragement of those I have brought up,
and truly sought to nurture in the Lord. This has led
me to many serious considerations how the case may,
under present circumstances, be in any way met.

My conclusion is that, believing as we do in the Lord as our Saviour, one Holy Spirit as our Sanctifier, and one God and Father of us all, our points of union are surely strong; and if we are members of one living Church, and expect to be such for ever. we may profitably unite in some religious engagements here below.

The world, and the things of it, occupy us much, and they are rapidly passing away; it will be well if we occasionally set apart a time for *unitedly* attending to the things of Eternity. I therefore propose that we try the following plan: if it answer, continue it; if not, by no means feel bound to it. That our party, in the first instance, should consist of no others than our children, and such grandchildren as may be old enough to attend. That our objects in meeting be for the strengthening of our faith, for our advancement in a religious and holy life, and for the promoting of Christian love and fellowship.

I propose that we read the Scriptures unitedly, in an easy, familiar manner, each being perfectly at liberty to make any remark or ask any questions. That it should be a time for religious instruction, by seeking to understand the mind of the Lord, for doctrine and practice, in searching the Scriptures, and bringing ourselves and our deeds to the light. . . . That either before or after the Scriptures are read we should consider how far we are engaged for the good of our fellow-men, and what, as far as we can judge, most conduces to this object. All the members of this little community are advised to communicate anything they may have found useful or interesting in religious books, and to bring forward anything that is doing for the good of mankind in the world generally.

I hope that thus meeting together may stimulate the family to more devotion of heart to the service of their God; at home and abroad to mind their different callings, however varied; and to be active in helping others. It is proposed that this meeting should take place once a month at each house in rotation. I now have drawn some little outline of what I desire, and if any of you like to unite with me in making the experiment, it would be very gratifying to me; still I hope all will feel at liberty to do as they think best themselves. Your dearly attached mother,

ELIZABETH FRY.

None but a parent whose spiritual life was pure, true, and deep, could feel such a constant solicitude about the spiritual progress and education of her family. Nor was this solicitude confined to the membership of her own circle. All who in any way assisted in her special department of philanthropy were councilled, wisely and kindly, to *act* rather than *preach* the gospel of Christ. In communications of this sort we find the newly-appointed matrons to the convict-ships advised to show their faith more by conduct than profession ; to avoid "religious cant;" to be prudent and circumspect ; to have discretion, wisdom and meekness. So she passed through life; the faithful friend, the patient, wise mother, the meek, tender wife, the succorer of all in distress. Everyone felt free to go to her with their troubles ; a reverse of circumstances, a sick child, a bad servant, or turn of sickness, all called forth her ready aid, and her wise, far-seeing judgment. And even in the last months of her life, when, worn out with service and pain, she was slowly going down to the gates of death, her children and grand-children were cut off suddenly by scarlet fever, she bowed resignedly to the Hand which had sent "sorrow upon sorrow." And when she who had been as a tower of strength to all around her, was reduced to the weakness of childhood by intense suffering, the survivors clung yet more closely to her, as if they could *not* let her go. So as physical strength declined, she actually grew stronger and brighter in mental and moral power. The deep and pain-ful tribulations which characterized her later years, but refined and purified the gold of her nature.

CHAPTER XIII.

COLLATERAL GOOD WORKS.

It must be remembered that Mrs. Fry's goodness was many-sided. Her charity did not
expend itself wholly on prisons and lunatic
asylums. It is right that, once in a while,
characters of such superlative excellence should
appear in our midst. Right, because otherwise
the light of charity would grow dim, the distinguishing graces of Christianity, flat and self-
ish, and individual faith be obscured in the
lapse of years, or the follies and fashions of
modern life. Such saints were Elizabeth of
Hungary, around whose name legend and story
have gathered, crowning her memory with
beauty ; Catherine of Sienna, who was honored
by the whole Christian Church of the fourteenth
century, and canonized for her goodness; and
Sarah Martin, the humble dressmaker of Yar-
mouth, who, in later times, has proved how
possible it is to render distinguished service in
the cause of humanity by small and lowly be-
ginnings, ultimately branching out into unex-

pected and remarkable ramifications. One can almost number such saints of modern life on the fingers ; but for all that, their examples have stimulated a host of lesser lights who still keep alive the savor of Christianity in our midst ; and towering above all her contemporaries in the grandeur of her deeds and words, Mrs. Fry still lives in song and story.

Among the collateral good works which she instituted and carried on, the first in order of time, and possibly of importance, as leading to all the others, was the "Association for the Improvement of Female Prisoners at Newgate." As this association and its objects were fully treated of in a previous chapter, it is unnecessary to enlarge upon it here. It suffices to say that it sought the welfare of the female prisoners during their detention in prison, and, also, to form in them such habits as should fit them for respectable life upon their discharge. Out of twelve ladies forming the original association started in 1817, eleven were Quakeresses.

Nearly akin to this society, was that for "The Improvement of Prison Discipline and Reformation of Juvenile Offenders." This society aimed at a two-fold object : first, by correspondence and deputations to awaken the minds of provincial magistrates and prison officials to the necessity for new arrangements, rules, and accommodations for prisoners; while it afforded watchful oversight and assistance to the numerous class of juvenile offenders who, after conviction, were absolutely thrown friendless upon the country, to continue and develop a course of crime. At the time of the formation of this society, public meetings were first held to further the welfare of prisoners, and to prevent the increase of crime. The doctrine of "stopping the supplies" first began to be understood; while even the most confirmed stickler for conservation could understand that there could not be a constant succession of old or middle-aged criminals to be dealt with by the law, provided the young were reformed, and trained in the ways of honesty. At one meeting, held at the Freemasons' Hall in 1821, in order to further the work of this society, Lord John Russell made an eloquent speech, concluding with the almost prophetic words: "Our country is now about to be distinguished for triumphs, the effect of which shall be to save, and not to destroy. Instead of laying waste the provinces of our enemies, we may begin now to reap a more solid glory in the reform of abuses at home, and in spreading happiness through millions of our population."

A society possessing broader aims, and working in a wider field, was the "British Ladies'

Society for Promoting the Reformation of Female Prisoners," formed in 1821, and really an outgrowth of Mrs Fry's efforts to *reclaim* the women whom she *taught* while in prison. It existed as a central point for communication and assistance between the various associations in Great Britain engaged in visiting prisons. Its corresponding committee also maintained interchanges of ideas and communications with those ladies on the Continent who were interested in the subject.

The Convict Ship Committee looked after the welfare of those who were transported, saw to the arrangements on board ship, the appointment of matrons, furnished employment, and secured shelters in the colonies, so that on arriving at the port of disembarkation the poor convicts should possess some sort of a place into which they could go. Further details of this branch of work will be given in the next chapter.

The chief work of the society, however, lay in providing homes for discharged female criminals. In 1824, "Homes" or "Shelters" were opened at Dublin, Liverpool, and many other places in England, Scotland, and the Continent. Tothill Fields Asylum, a small home for some of the most hopeful of the discharged prisoners, was opened at Westminster. Miss Neave, a charitable Christian lady, was fired with some of Mrs. Fry's enthusiasm, and devoted both time and money to the carrying out of the project. She relates that the idea first entered her mind when out driving one morning with Mrs. Fry. That lady, speaking of her work, said, in somewhat saddened tones: "Often have I known the career of a promising young woman, charged with a first offence, to end in a condemned cell. Were there but a refuge for the young offender, my work would be less painful." As the result, Tothill Fields Asylum was opened, with four inmates. Very soon, nine were accommodated, and within a few years, under the new name of "The Royal Manor Hall Asylum," it sheltered fifty women of different ages.

Another class of discharged prisoners, viz., little girls, were also provided for by this society. To these were added destitute girls, who had not yet found their way into prison ; and the whole number were placed under judicious training in a "School for Discipline," at Chelsea. This institution became most successful in training these children up in orderly and respectable habits. At one time Mrs. Fry endeavored to get this home under Government rule, but Sir Robert Peel considered that the ends of humanity would be better served by keeping it under the control of, and supported by, private individuals.

A temporary stay at Brighton suggested the formation of the District Visiting Society. This aimed, not at indiscriminate alms-giving, but at "the encouragement of industry and frugality among the poor by visits at their own habitations ; the relief of real distress, whether arising from sickness or other causes, and the prevention of mendicity and imposture." Visitors were appointed, who went from house to house among the poor, encouraging habits of thrift and cleanliness ; whilst a savings bank received deposits, and trained these same poor to save for the inevitable "rainy day."

Probably one of the most extensive works of benevolence and good-will carried on to success by Mrs. Fry, next to her prison labors, was the establishment of libraries for the men of the Coast Guard Service. This arose from a circumstance which occurred during the sojourn at Brighton, for the benefit of her somewhat shattered health, in 1824.

During her residence there she was subject to distressing attacks of faintness in the night and early morning. Again and again, it was necessary to immediately throw open her chamber window for the admission of the fresh air ; and always upon such occasions the figure of a

solitary coast-guardsman was to be seen pacing
the beach, on the look-out for smugglers.
Such a post, and such a service, presenting as it
did a life of hardship and danger, inevitably
attracted her sympathetic attention ; and she
began to take an almost unconscious interest in
the affairs of this man. Shortly after, when
driving out, she stopped the carriage and spoke
to one of the men at the station. He replied
civilly, that the members of the Preventive Service were not allowed to hold any conversation
with strangers, and requested to be excused
from saying any more. Mrs. Fry, feeling somewhat fearful that her kindness might bring him
into difficulty with his superiors, gave the man
her card, and desired him to tell the man in
command of the station that she had spoken to
him with the sole object of inquiring after the
welfare of the men and their families. A few
days afterwards, the lieutenant who commanded
at that post waited upon Mrs. Fry, and, contrary to her fears, welcomed her inquiries as
auguries of good. He confessed to her that the
officers, men, women, and children, all suffered
much from loneliness, privation, semi-banish-
ment — for the stations were mostly placed in
dreary and inaccessible places — unpopularity
with the surrounding people, and harassment by
constant watching, through all weather, for

smugglers. The nature and regulations of the
Coast Blockade of Preventive Service precluded
anything like visiting or *personal* kindness.
There was really no way of benefiting them
except by providing them with literature calculated to promote their intellectual and religious
good, besides furnishing an occupation for the
dreary, lonely hours which fell to their portion.
This course Mrs. Fry immediately adopted.

She first applied to the British and Foreign
Bible Society ; the Committee responded with
a grant of fifty Bibles and twenty-five Testaments. These were distributed to the men on
the stations in that district, and most gratefully
received. As a proof of the gratitude of the
recipients, the following little note was sent to
Mrs. Fry by the commanding officer : —

My Dear Madam,— Happy am I in being able to
make you acquainted with the unexpected success I have
met with in my attempt to forward, among the seamen
employed on the coast, your truly laudable and benevolent desire — the dissemination of the Holy Scriptures.
I have made a point of seeing Lieutenant H., who has
promised me that if you will extend your favors to
Dutchmere, he will distribute the books, and carefully
attend to the performance of Divine service on the Sabbath Day. Also Lieutenant D., who will shortly have a
command in this division. I trust, Madam, I shall be
still further able to forward those views, which must, to
all who embrace them, prove a sovereign balm in the

hour of death and the day of judgment. With respectful compliments to the ladies, allow me to remain, dear
Madam, your devoted servant.

This communication enclosed another little
note from the seamen, which expressed their
feelings as follows : —

We, the seamen of Salt Dean Station, have the pleasure to announce to those ladies whose goodness has
pleased them to provide the Bibles and Testaments for
the use of us seamen, that we have received them. We
do therefore return our most hearty thanks for the same ;
and we do assure the ladies whose friendship has proved
so much in behalf of seamen, that every care shall
be taken of the said books ; and, at the same time, great
care shall be taken to instruct those who have not the
gift of education, and we at any time shall feel a pleasure
in doing the same.

Some ten years later, when visiting in the
Isle of Wight, she conceived the plan of extending the system by supplying libraries to all the
Coast Guard stations in the United Kingdom.
The magnitude of the work may be realized
when we state that there were about 500
stations, including within their boundaries some
21,000 men, women and children. How to set
about the work was her next anxiety, for it
seemed useless to attempt it without at least
£1,000 in hand. She submitted the proposition
to Lord Althorp, at that time Chancellor of the

Exchequer, and asked for a grant of £500 from Government, in order to supplement the £1,000 which she hoped to raise by private subscriptions. A grant could not, however, be made at that time on account of different political considerations; but within a few months one was obtained, and her heart rejoiced at this new proof of appreciation of her work on the part of those high in office. An entry in her journal in February, 1835, reads thus :—

The way appears opening with our present Ministers to obtain libraries for all the Coast Guard stations, a matter I have long had at heart. My desire is to do all these things with a single eye to the glory of God, and the welfare of my fellow mortals; and if they succeed, to pray that He alone who can bless and increase, may prosper the work of my unworthy hands. Upon going to the Custom House, I found Government had at last granted my request, and given £500 for libraries for the stations; this is, I think, cause for thankfulness.

Private subscriptions were sedulously sought, and large sums flowed in ; besides these, many large book-sellers, and the chief religious publishing societies gave donations of books. These were valued in the aggregate at about one thousand pounds. The details of the work were left to herself, while the Rev. John W. Cunningham, Captain W. E. Parry, and Captain Bowles selected the books.

The total number of volumes for the stations amounted to 25,896. Each station possessed a library of fifty-two different books, while each *district*, which included the stations in that part of the country, possessed a larger assortment for reference and exchange. Most of the parcels were sent, carriage free, in Government vessels, by means of the Custom House. This work involved many journeys to London, and much arduous labor. The Rev. Thomas Timpson, a dissenting minister in London, acted most efficiently as secretary, and lightened her labors to a large extent. During the summer of 1835, the work of distributing these volumes was nearly all accomplished ; and as during that summer Mr. Fry's business demanded his presence in the south of England, she decided to seize the opportunity of visiting all the Coast Guard stations in that part of the country. In this way she journeyed along the whole south coast, from the Forelands to Land's End, welcomed everywhere with true-hearted veneration and love. She addressed herself principally to the commanders of the different stations, bespeaking for the books care in treatment and regularity in carrying out the exchanges. These gentlemen manifested the warmest interest in the plan, and promised their most thorough co-operation.

At Portsmouth she visited the Haslar Hospital, and while in Portsea, the female Penitentiary. In the latter institution she desired to speak a few words to the inmates, who were, accordingly, assembled in the parlor for the purpose. Mrs. Fry laid her bonnet on the table, sat down, and made different inquiries about the conduct of the young women, and the rules enforced. It appeared that two of them were pointed out as being peculiarly hardened and refractory. She did not, however, notice this at the time, but delivered a short and affectionate address to all. Afterwards, on going away, she went up to the two refractory ones, and, extending her hand to them, said to each, most impressively : " I trust I shall hear better things of thee." Both of them burst into unexpected tears, thus acknowledging the might of kindness over such natures.

At Falmouth, during this same excursion, she supplied some of the men-of-war with libraries. Some of the packets participated in the same boon, so that each ship sailing from that port took out a well-chosen library of about thirty books. These library books were changed on each succeeding voyage, and were highly appreciated by both officers and seamen.

In 1836, the report of the Committee for furnishing the Coast Guard of the United Kingdom with Libraries, appeared. From it, we find that in addition to the £500 kindly granted by the Government at first towards the project, Mr. Spring Rice, a later Chancellor of the Exchequer granted further sums amounting to £460. Thus the undertaking was brought to a successful termination. There were supplied : 498 libraries for the stations on shore, including 25,896 volumes ; 74 libraries for districts on shore, including 12,880 volumes ; 48 libraries for cruisers, including 1,876 volumes ; school books for children of crews, 6,464 volumes ; pamphlets, tracts, etc., 5,357 numbers ; total, 52,464 volumes and numbers.

These were distributed among 21,000 people on Coast Guard stations, and to the hands on board many ships. Years afterwards, many and very unexpected letters of thanks continued to reach Mrs. Fry from those who had benefited by this good work.

" Instant in season and out of season," this very trip in the south of England produced another good work. She, with her husband and daughter, returned home by way of North Devon, Somerset, and Wiltshire. At Amesbury she tarried long enough to learn something of the mental destitution of the shepherds employed on' Salisbury Plain, and set her fertile brain to contrive a scheme for the supply of the necessary books. She communicated her desires and intentions to the clergyman of the parish, and Sir Edward and Lady Antrobus, who unitedly undertook to furnish a librarian. A short note from this individual, addressed to Mrs. Fry some few months after, proved how well the thing was working. In it he said: "Forty-five books are in constant circulation, with the additional magazines. More than fifty poor people read them with attention, return them with thanks, and desire the loan of more, frequently observing that they think it a very kind thing indeed that they should be furnished with so many good books, free of all costs, so entertaining and instructive, these long winter evenings."

About the same period Mrs. Fry formed a Servants' Society for the succor and help of domestic servants. She had known instances wherein so many of this class had come to sorrow, in every sense, for the lack of temporary refuge and assistance, that she alone undertook to found this institution. In an entry made in her journal in 1825, we find the following reference to this matter: —

The Servants' Society appears gradually opening as if it would be established according to my desire. No one knows what I go through in forming these institutions; it is always in fear, and mostly with many misgivings, wondering at myself for doing it. I believe the original motive is love to my Master and love to my fellow-creatures; but fear is so predominant a feeling in my mind that it makes me suffer, perhaps unnecessarily, from doubts. I felt something like freedom in prayer before making the regulations of the Servants' Society. Sometimes my natural understanding seems enlightened about things of that kind, as if I were helped to see the right and useful thing.

In closing this chapter, some allusion must be made to her latest effort. It dates from 1840, and owed its foundation principally to her. It was that of the "Nursing Sisters," an order called into existence by the needs of every-day life. As she visited in sick-chambers, or ministered to the needs of the poor, she felt the want of efficient skilled nurses, and, with the restless energy of a true philanthropist, set about remedying the want. Her own leisure would not admit of training a band of nurses, but her desire was carried into effect by Mrs. Samuel Gurney, her sister-in-law. Under this lady's supervision, and the patronage of the Queen Dowager, Lady Inglis, and other members of the nobility, a number of young women were selected, trained, and taught to fulfil the duties of nurses. They were placed for some time in the largest public hospitals, in order to learn the scientific system of nursing; then, supposing their qualifications and conduct were found to be

satisfactory, they were received permanently as
Sisters. These Sisters wore a distinctive dress,
received an annual stipend of about twenty
guineas, and were provided with a home during
the intervals of their engagements. There was
also a " Superannuation Fund " for the relief of
those Sisters who should, after long service, fall
into indigence or ill-health. Christian women,
of all denominations, were encouraged to join
the institution ; while the services of the Sisters
were equally available in the palace and in the
cottage. No Sister was permitted to receive
presents, directly or indirectly, from the patients
nursed by her, seeing that all sums received
went to a common fund for the benefit of the
Society. These Sisters appear to have worked
very much like the modern deaconesses of the
Church of England. They rightly earned the
title of " Sisters of Mercy."

These are but examples of Mrs. Fry's good
works,— done "all for love, and none for a
reward."

Many other smaller works claimed her
thoughts, so that her life was very full of the
royal grace of charity. The list might have
been still further extended, but to the ordinary
student of her life it is already sufficiently long
to prove the reality of her religion and her love.

CHAPTER XIV.

It is an old adage that "nothing succeeds like success." Mrs. Fry and her prison labors had become famous; not only famous, but the subjects of talk, both in society and out of it. Kings, queens, statesmen, philanthropists, ladies of fashion, devotees of charity, authors and divines were all looking with more or less interest at the experiments made by the apostles of this new crusade against vice, misery, and crime. Many of them courted acquaintance with the Quakeress who hesitated not to plunge into gloomy prison-cells, nor to penetrate pest-houses decimated with jail fever, in pursuance of her mission. And while they courted her acquaintance, they fervently wished her " God speed." Two or three communications, still in existence, prove that Hannah More and Maria Edgeworth were of the number of good wishers. In a short note written from Barley Wood,

in 1826, Hannah More thus expressed her appreciation of Mrs. Fry's character:—

Any request of yours, if within my very limited power,
cannot fail to be immediately complied with. In your
kind note, I wish you had mentioned something of your
own health and that of your family. I look back with no
small pleasure to the too short visits with which you
once indulged me; a repetition of it would be no little
gratification to me. Whether Divine Providence may
grant it or not, I trust through Him who loved us, and
gave Himself for us, that we may hereafter meet in that
blessed country where there is neither sin, sorrow, nor
separation.

Many years previous to this, Hannah More
had presented Mrs. Fry with a copy of her
Practical Piety, writing this inscription on the
fly-leaf :—

To MRS. FRY. Presented by Hannah More, as a
token of veneration of her heroic zeal, Christian charity,
and persevering kindness to the most forlorn of human
beings. They were naked, and she clothed them; in
prison, and she visited them; ignorant, and she taught
them, for *His* sake, in *His* name, and by *His* word, who
went about doing good.

No words can add to the beauty of this inscription.

During one of Maria Edgeworth's London
visits, the name and fame of Mrs. Fry, and
Newgate as civilized by her, formed such an
attraction that the lively Irish authoress must

needs go to see for herself.   In her picturesque
style she thus affords us an account of her
visit : —

Yesterday we went, the moment we had swallowed our
breakfast, by appointment to Newgate.   The private door
opened at sight of our tickets, and the great doors, and
the little doors, and the thick doors, and doors of all
sorts, were unbolted and unlocked, and on we went,
through dreary but clean passages, till we came to a
room where rows of empty benches fronted us, and a
table, on which lay a large Bible.   Several ladies and
gentlemen entered, and took their seats on benches, at
either side of the table, in silence.

Enter Mrs. Fry, in a drab-colored silk cloak, and plain,
borderless Quaker cap ; a most benevolent countenance ;
Guido Madonna face, calm, benign.   " I must make an
inquiry ; is Maria Edgeworth here ?   And where ? "   I
went forward ; she bade us come and sit beside her.   Her
first smile, as she looked upon me, I can never forget.
The prisoners came in, and in an orderly manner ranged
themselves on the benches.   All quite clean faces, hair,
caps and hands.   On a very low bench in front, little
children were seated, and watched by their mothers.   Almost all these women, about thirty, were under sentence
of transportation ; some few only were for imprisonment.
One who did not appear was under sentence of death ;
frequently women, when sentenced to death, become ill,
and unable to attend Mrs. Fry ; the others come regularly
and voluntarily.

She opened the Bible, and read in the most sweetly
solemn, sedate voice I ever heard, slowly and distinctly,
without anything in the manner that could distract attention from the matter.   Sometimes she paused to explain,

which she did with great judgment, addressing the convicts — " *We* have felt! *We* are convinced ! " They
were very attentive, unexpectedly interested, I thought,
in all she said, and touched by her manner. There was
nothing put on in their countenances; not any appearance of hypocrisy. I studied their countenances carefully, but I could not see any which, without knowing to
whom they belonged, I should have decided was bad;
yet Mrs. Fry assured me that all those women had been
of the worst sort. She confirmed what we have read and
heard — that it was by their love of their children that
she first obtained influence over these abandoned women.
When she first took notice of one or two of their fine
children, the mothers said that if she could but save
their children from the misery they had gone through in
vice, they would do anything she bid them. And when
they saw the change made in their children by her school-
ing, they begged to attend themselves. I could not have
conceived that the love of their children could have
remained so strong in hearts in which every other feeling
of virtue had so long been dead. The Vicar of Wakefield's sermon in prison is, it seems, founded on a deep
and true knowledge of human nature; the spark of good
is often smothered, never wholly extinguished. Mrs.
Fry often says an extempore prayer; but this day she
was quite silent; while she covered her face with her
hands for some minutes, the women were perfectly silent,
with their eyes fixed upon her; and when she said, " You
may go," they went away *slowly*. The children sat quite
still the whole time; when one leaned, her mother behind
her sat her upright. Mrs. Fry told us that the dividing
the women into classes, and putting them under monitors,
had been of the greatest advantage. There is some little
pecuniary advantage attached to the office of monitor

which makes them emulous to obtain it. We went through the female wards with Mrs. Fry, and saw the women at various works, knitting, rug-making, etc. They have done a great deal of needle-work very neatly, and some very ingenious. When I expressed my foolish wonder at this to Mrs. Fry's sister, she replied, " We have to do, recollect, Ma'am, not with fools, but with rogues." . . . . Far from being disappointed with the sight of what Mrs. Fry has done, I was delighted.

This *naïve,* informal chronicle of a visit to Newgate incidentally lets out the fact that the gloomy prison was fast becoming attractive to visitors — indeed, quite a show-place. That Mrs. Fry's labors were receiving official honor and recognition also, there is plenty of evidence to prove. In Prussia, her principles and exhortations had made such headway that the Government was adapting old prisons and building new, in order to carry out the modern doctrines of classification and employment. In Denmark, the King had given his sanction to the measures proposed by the Royal Danish Chancery for adding new buildings to the prison. As soon as these buildings were completed the females would be separated from the males, female warders were to be appointed, employment found for all prisoners, and books of information and devotion were to be supplied to each cell; while a chaplain (an unknown official, hitherto) was to be appointed. In Germany, four new

penitentiaries were to be constructed ; viz ,
at Berlin, Münster in Westphalia, Ratibor in
Silesia, and Königsberg. Two of these penitentiaries were to be exactly like the Model
Prison at Pentonville ; separate confinement
was to be practically carried out, and the prisoners were to be taught trades under the superintendence of picked teachers. From Düsseldorf
came information that all the female prisoners
were improving under the new *régime;* that an
asylum for discharged prisoners was effecting a
wonderful transformation in the characters and
lives of those who sought refuge there ; and
that the inmates only left its shelter to secure
situations in service. In addition to these
cheering items she had the satisfaction of holding communications with many princely, noble
and royal personages on the Continent, respecting the progress of her favorite work, and the
new regulations and buildings then adopted.

To return to her home-work and its ramifications will only be to prove how far the great
principles which she had taught were bearing
fruit. The Government Inspectors were working hard upon the lines laid down by Mrs. Fry;
and if at times they found anything which clashed
with their own pre-conceived ideas of what a
prison should be, they were always ready to
make allowance for the difficulties of pioneer

work, such as this lady and her coadjutors had
to do at Newgate. At Paramatta, New South
Wales, where, according to a letter from the
Rev. Samuel Marsden in an earlier part of this
work, the condition of female convicts had been
scandalous to the Government which shipped
them out there, and deplorable in the extreme for the poor creatures themselves, a large
factory had been erected, designed for the reception of the convicts upon their landing. It
served its purpose well, being commodious
enough to receive not only the new importa-
tions, but the refractory women also, who were
returned from their situations. It was well
managed ; the inmates being divided into three
classes, and treated with more or less kindness
accordingly. True, at one time, even after the
erection of this factory, from the management
being entrusted to inefficient hands, a scene of
disorder and misrule had prevailed ; but that
had been promptly and firmly repressed. Hard
labor and strict discipline had succeeded in re-
ducing the temporary confusion to something
like order, and made residence there the dread
of returning evil-doers, whilst it afforded a refuge for new-comers. Sir Richard Bourke, and
Sir Ralph and Lady Darling, used every endeavor to make the place a success ; while, at
home, Lord Glenelg and Sir George Grey gave

the matter, on behalf of the Government, every needful and possible aid. A good superinten-dent and matron were appointed from England, and supplied with every requisite for the in-struction and occupation of the convicts at the factory.

This cordial co-operation of the Colonial Of-fice in her schemes of improvement for the female convicts at Paramatta, encouraged her to attempt the same good work for the convicts at Hobart Town, Tasmania. It happened that by 1843 the transportation of females to New South Wales had ceased, the younger establish-ment at Hobart Town receiving all the female convicts ; but, like the hydra of classic lore, the evil sprang up there as fresh and as vigorous as if it had not been conquered at Paramatta. Lady Franklin and other ladies communicated with Mrs. Fry, showing her the great need that still existed for her benevolent exertions in that quarter. From these communications it seemed that the assignment of women into domestic slavery still continued, in all its dire forms. When a convict ship arrived from England, em-ployers of all grades became candidates for the services of the convicts. With the exception of publicans, and ticket-of-leave men, who were not allowed to employ convicts, anybody and everybody might engage the poor banished

prisoners without any guarantee whatsoever as
to the future conduct of the employer toward the
servant, or specification as to the kind of work
to be performed. Those convicts who have behaved themselves best on the voyage out were
assigned to the best classes of society, while
the others fell to the refuse of the employers'
class. As it was a fact that a large proportion
of the tradesmen applying for servants were
convicts who had fully served their time, it may
be imagined how lacking in civilization and integrity such employers often were. But if the
condition of the convicts was hopeless after their
assignment to places of service, it was, if possible, more hopeless still in the home, or " factory," in which they were first received. Some
of the letters before referred to cast a flood of
terrible light upon the condition of the poor
wretches who had quitted their country "for
that country's good," even when under supposed
discipline and restraint. A passage from one of
these letters reads like an ugly story of "the
good old times ! "

The Cascade Factory is a receiving-house for the
women on their first arrival (if not assigned from the
ship), or on their transition from one place to another, and
also a house of correction for faults committed in domestic service ; but with no pretension to be a place of reformatory discipline, and seldom failing to turn out the

women worse than they entered it. Religious instruction there was none, except that occasionally on the
Sabbath the superintendent of the prison read prayers,
and sometimes divine service was performed by a chaplain, who also had an extensive parish to attend to.

The officers of the establishment consisted, at that
time, of only five persons — a porter, the superintendent,
and matron, and two assistants. The number of persons
in the factory, when first visited by Miss Hayter, was five
hundred and fifty. It followed, of course, that nothing
like prison discipline could be enforced, or even attempted. In short, so congenial to its inmates was this
place of custody (it would be unfair to call it a place of
punishment) that they returned to it again and again
when they wished to change their place of servitude;
and they were known to commit offences on purpose to
be sent into it, preparatory to their| reassignment else-
where.

Yet, after visiting the factory, and hearing everybody
speak of its unhappy inmates, I could not but feel that
they were far more to be pitied than blamed. No one
has ever attempted any measure to ameliorate their degraded condition. I felt that had they had the opportunity of religious instruction, some at least might be
rescued. I wish I could express to you all I feel and
think upon the subject, and how completely I am over-
whelmed with the awful sin of allowing so many wretched
beings to perish for lack of instruction. Even in the
hospital of the factory the unhappy creatures are as
much neglected, in spiritual things, as if they were in a
heathen land. There are no Bibles, and no Christians to
tell them of a Saviour's dying love.

Mrs. Fry laid these communications before
the Colonial Secretary without delay, praying

him to alter this terrible state of things. She
was at once listened to. The building was
altered, by orders from England; the convicts
were divided into classes; employment and
discipline were provided; daily instruction, both
secular and religious, was imparted; so that,
by degrees, the establishment became what it
should have been from the first—a house of
detention, discipline, and refuge. In addition,
a large vessel called the *Anson* was fitted up as
a temporary prison, sent out to Hobart Town,
and moored in the river. This vessel received
the new shipments of transports from England,
and afforded, by its staff of officers, opportunity
for a six months' training of the convicts, who
then were not permitted to enter the service of
the colonists until after this period had expired.
By these different means Mrs. Fry had the
satisfaction of knowing that the convicts had
yet another opportunity of amendment granted
them after leaving the prisons of their native
land. It has already been observed that in
most of the prisons of the United Kingdom
female warders were employed, while matrons
were appointed on the out-going convict ships.
Contrary to the lot of many reformers, Mrs.
Fry was spared to see most of the reforms
which she had recommended, become law.

After Mrs. Fry's death an interesting report

was issued by the Inspector-General of Prisons in Ireland, relating to the Grange Gorman Lane Female Prison, Dublin. Mrs. Fry had taken special interest in this prison, it having been the first erected *exclusively for women* in the United Kingdom, and intended, if found successful, to serve as a sort of model for other places. The experiment had proved entirely successful and satisfactory; matron, warders and chaplain all united in one chorus of praise. Major Cottingham, the Inspector-General, wrote: —

Although I made my annual inspection of this prison on February 18th, 1847, as a date upon which to form my report, yet I have had very many opportunities of seeing it during past and former years, in my duties connected with my superintendence of the convict department. The visitors may see many changes in the faces and persons of the prisoners, but no surprise can ever find a difference in the high and superior order with which this prison is conducted. The matron, Mrs. Rawlins, upon whom the entire responsibility of the interior management devolves, was selected some years since, and sent over to this country by the benevolent and philanthropic Mrs. Fry, whose exertions in the cause of female prison reformation were extended to all parts of the British Empire, and who, although lately summoned to the presence of her Divine Master, has nowhere left a more valuable instance of her sound judgment and high discriminating powers than in the selection of Mrs. Rawlins to be placed at the head of this experimental prison, occupied alone by females; and so successful has the experiment been, that I understand several other prisons solely for females have been lately opened in Scotland, and even in Australia. In this prison is to be seen an uninterrupted system of reformatory discipline in every class, such as is to be found in no other prison that I am aware of.

The matron alluded to in the above extracts gratefully acknowledged that Mrs. Fry's plan had completely succeeded in every respect, while she was equally grateful in owning that to her instructions and wise maternal counsel she herself owed her own fitness for that special branch of the work.

The testimonies to her success not only came in from official quarters, but from the prisoners themselves. This chronicle would scarcely be complete without a specimen or two of the many communications she received from prisoners at home and from convicts abroad. True, on one or two occasions the women at Newgate had behaved in a somewhat refractory manner, for their poor degraded human nature could not conceive of pure disinterested Christian love working for their good without fee or reward ; but even at these times their better nature very soon reasserted itself, and penitence and tears took the place of insubordination. To those who had sinned against and had been forgiven by her, Mrs. Fry's memory was something

almost too holy for earth. No orthodoxly canonized saint of the Catholic Church ever received
truer reverence, or performed such miracles of
moral healing.

The following communication reached her
from some of the prisoners at Newgate:—

HONORED MADAM,— Influenced by gratitude to our
general benefactress and friend, we humbly venture to
address you. It is with sorrow we say that we had not
the pleasure of seeing you at the accustomed time, which
we have always been taught to look for—we mean Fri-
day last. We are fearful that your health was the cause
of our being deprived of that heartfelt joy which your
presence always diffuses through the prison; but we
hope, through the mercies of God, we shall be able personally to return you the grateful acknowledgments of
our hearts, before we leave our country forever, for all
the past and present favors so benevolently bestowed
upon what has been termed the "most unfortunate of
society," until cheered by your benevolence, kindness and
charity: and hoping that your health, which is so dear to
such a number of unfortunates, will be fully re-estab-
lished before we go, so that after our departure from our
native land, those who are so unfortunate as to fall into
our situation may enjoy the same blessing, both temporally and spiritually, that we have done before them.
And may our minds be impressed with a due sense of
the many comforts we have enjoyed whilst under your
kind protection. Honored and worthy Madam, we hope
we shall be pardoned for our presumption in addressing
you at this time, but our fears of not seeing you before
the time of our departure induce us to entreat your
acceptance of our prayers for your restoration to your

family; and may the prayers and supplications of the unfortunate prisoners ascend to Heaven for the prolonging
of that life which is so dear to the most wretched of the
English nation. Honored Madam, we beg leave to subscribe ourselves, with humble respect, your most grateful
and devoted,

THE PRISONERS OF NEWGATE.

The following letter was from a convict at
Paramatta, New South Wales, some time after
her banishment to that colony :—

HONORED MADAM, — The duty I owe to you, likewise
to the benevolent society to which you have the honor
to belong, compels me to take up my pen to return you
my most sincere thanks for the heavenly instruction I
derived from you, and the dear friends, during my confinement in Newgate.

In the month of April, 1817, that blessed prayer of
yours sank deep into my heart; and as you said, so I
have found it, that when no eyes see and no ears hear,
God both sees and hears, and then it was that the
arrow of conviction entered my hard heart; in Newgate
it was that poor Harriet, like the Prodigal Son, came to
herself, and took with her words, and sought the Lord.
Truly I can say with David, "Before I was afflicted I
went astray, but now I have learned Thy ways, O Lord."
. . . Believe me, my dear Madam, I bless the day that
brought me inside Newgate walls, for then it was that
the ways of Divine truth shone into my dark mind. . . .
Believe me, my dear Madam, although I am a poor captive in a distant land, I would not give up having communion with God one single day for my liberty; for what
is the liberty of the body compared with the liberty of

the soul? Soon will the time come when death will release me from all the earthly fetters that hold me now, for I trust to be with Christ, who bought me with His precious blood. And now, my dear Madam, these few sincere sentiments of mine I wish you to make known to the world, that the world may see that your labor in Newgate has not been in vain in the Lord. Please give my love to the dear friends; the keeper of Newgate, and all the afflicted prisoners; and although we may never meet on earth again, I hope we shall all meet in the realms of bliss, never to part again.

Believe me to remain your humble servant,

HARRIET S——.

In addition to the grateful acknowledgments of "those who were ready to perish," Mrs. Fry won an unusual meed of honorable esteem from the noble and great. Sovereigns and rulers, statesmen and cabinet councillors, all owned the worth of goodness, and rendered to the Quaker lady the homage of both tongue and heart. Beside that notable visit to the Mansion House to be presented to Queen Charlotte, in 1818, Mrs. Fry had many interviews with royalty—these royal and noble personages conferring honor upon themselves more than upon her by their kindly interest in her work.

In 1822 the Prince and Princess Royal of Denmark visited England, and spent considerable time in inspecting public institutions, schools, and charities tending to advance the general well-being of the people. Of course Mrs. Fry's name was spoken of prominently, seeing that she was then in the full tide of her Newgate labors. The Duchess of Gloucester first introduced Mrs. Fry to the Princess, when a few words of question and explanation were given in relation to the prison enterprise. But some days later, the family at Plashet House were apprised of the fact that the Princess intended honoring them with her company at breakfast. She came at the hour appointed, and, while partaking of their hospitality, entered fully into Mrs. Fry's work, learning of her those particulars which she could not otherwise gain. The foundation of a firm friendship with the Princess Royal of Denmark was thus laid, which continued through all Mrs. Fry's after life.

In 1831 she obtained her first interview with our gracious Queen, then the young Princess Victoria. Then, as now, the Royal Family of England was always interested in works of charity and philanthropy, and the young Princess displayed the early bent of her mind in this interview. In the most unaffected style Mrs. Fry thus tells the story: "About three weeks ago I paid a very satisfactory visit to the Duchess of Kent, and her very pleasing daughter, the Princess Victoria. William Allen went with me. We took some books on the subject of slavery, with the hope of influencing the young Princess in that important cause. We were received with much kindness and cordiality, and I felt my way open to express not only my desire that the best blessing may rest upon them, but that the young Princess might follow the example of our blessed Lord; that as she grew in stature she might also grow in favor with God and man. I also ventured to remind her of King Josiah, who began to reign at eight years old, and did that which was right in the sight of the Lord, turning neither to the right hand nor to the left, which seemed to be well received. Since that I thought it right to send the Duke of Gloucester my brother Joseph's work on the Sabbath, with a rather serious letter, and had a very valuable answer from him, full of feeling. I have an invitation to visit the Duchess of Gloucester the next Fourth Day. May good result to them and no harm to myself; but I feel those openings a rather weighty responsibility, and desire to be faithful and not forward. I had long felt an inclination to see the young Princess, and endeavor to throw a little weight into the right scale, seeing the very important place she is likely to fill. I was much pleased with her, and think her a sweet, lovely and hopeful child."

Some three years afterwards the Duke of

Gloucester died, and his death recalled the old times when he was quartered at Norwich with his regiment. The biographers of Elizabeth Fry tell us that the Duke "was amongst the few who addressed words of friendly caution and sound advice to the young and motherless sisters at Earlham." She never forgot the old friendship—a friendship which had been increased by the unfailing interest of both the Duke and Duchess in her philanthropic work. As soon as she heard of the bereavement she wrote the following letter to the Princess Sophia of Gloucester:—

My dear Friend:

I hope thou wilt not feel it an intrusion my expressing my sympathy with thee in the death of the Duke of Gloucester. To lose a dear and only brother is no small trial, and for a while makes the world appear very desolate. But I trust that having thy pleasant pictures marred in this life may be one means of opening brighter prospects in the life to come, and of having thy treasure increased in the heavenly inheritance. The Duchess of Gloucester kindly commissioned a lady to write to me, who gave me a very comforting account of the state of the Duke's mind. I feel it cause for much thankfulness that he was so sustained through faith in his Lord and Saviour; and we may humbly trust, through His merits, saved with an everlasting salvation. It would be very pleasant to me to hear how thy health and spirits are after so great a shock, and I propose inquiring at Blackheath, where I rather expect to be next week; or if thou wouldst have the kindness to request one of thy ladies in waiting to write me a few lines I should be much obliged. I hope that my dear and valued friend, the Duchess of Gloucester, is as well as we can expect after her deep affliction.

Shortly after this she paid a visit of condolence to the Duchess by appointment.

Early in 1840 the young Queen, her present Majesty, sent Mrs. Fry a present of fifty pounds by Lord Normanby for the Refuge at Chelsea, and appointed an audience. On the first day of February Mrs. Fry, accompanied by her brother, Samuel Gurney, and William Allen, attended at Buckingham Palace. This was only a few days before Her Majesty espoused Prince Albert. Mrs. Fry writes as follows in her journal, respecting that interview : —

We went to Buckingham Palace and saw the Queen. Our interview was short. Lord Normanby, the Home Secretary, presented us. The Queen asked us when we were going on the Continent. She said it was some years since she saw me. She asked about Caroline Neave's Refuge, for which she has lately sent me the fifty pounds. This gave me an opportunity of thanking her. I ventured to express my satisfaction that she encouraged various works of charity, and I said it reminded me of the words of Scripture, " With the merciful Thou wilt show Thyself merciful." Before we withdrew I stopped, and said I hoped the Queen would allow me to assure her that it was our prayer that the blessing of God might rest upon the Queen and her Consort.

In January, 1842, the Lady Mayoress pressed Mrs. Fry to attend a banquet given at the Mansion House, in order principally to meet Prince Albert, Sir Robert Peel, and the different Ministers of State. After a little mental conflict she decided to go, with the earnest hope and purpose of doing more good for the prisoners. A summary of her sayings and doings at that banquet is best supplied in her own words :—

I had an important conversation on a female prison being built, with Sir James Graham, our present Secretary of State. . . . I think it was a very important beginning with him for our British Ladies' Society. With Lord Aberdeen, Foreign Secretary, I spoke on some matters connected with the present state of the Continent; with Lord Stanley, our Colonial Secretary, upon the state of our penal colonies, and the condition of the women in them, hoping to open the door for further communications with him upon these subjects. Nearly the whole dinner was occupied in deeply interesting conversation with Prince Albert and Sir Robert Peel. With the Prince I spoke very seriously upon the Christian education of their children. . . . the infinite importance of a holy and religious life; how I had seen it in all ranks of life, no real peace or prosperity without it; then the state of Europe, the advancement of religion in the continental courts; then prisons, their present state in this country, my fear that our punishments were becoming too severe, my wish that the Queen should be informed of some particulars respecting separate confinement. We also had much entertaining conversation about my journeys, the state of Europe, modes of living, and habits of countries.

With Sir Robert Peel I dwelt much more on the prison subject; I expressed my fears that jailers had too much power, that punishment was rendered uncertain, and often too severe; pressed upon him the need of mercy, and begged him to see the new prison, and to have the dark cells a little altered. . . . I was wonderfully strengthened, bodily and mentally, and believe I was in my right place there, though an odd one for me. I sat between Prince Albert and Sir Robert Peel at dinner, and a most interesting time we had. . . . It was a very remarkable occasion; I hardly ever had such respect and kindness shown to me; it was really humbling and affecting to me, and yet sweet to see such various persons, whom I had worked with for years past, showing such genuine kindness and esteem so far beyond my most unworthy deserts.

Royalty and nobility thus concurred in carrying out, although perhaps unconsciously, the Scriptural command : " *Esteem such very highly in love for their works' sake.*" It is interesting to notice how very frequently, in this world, the course of events does coincide with the words of Holy Writ, and the honor which Providence showers upon a remarkable servant of God. It is equally interesting, also, to see how completely, in the philanthropic Quakeress, the nobility of moral greatness was acknowledged by the highest personages in the land.

Very soon after this meeting at the Mansion House, the King of Prussia arrived in England, to stand as sponsor to the infant Prince of Wales ; and, speedily after his arrival, he desired to see Mrs. Fry. He neither forgot nor ignored her visits to his dominions in the interests of charity ; and he concluded that a woman who could travel thousands of miles upon the Continent, in order to ameliorate the condition of prisoners and lunatics, must be worth visiting at her own home. By his special desire, therefore, she was sent for, to meet him at the Mansion House. After the dinner, at which no toasts were proposed, in deference to Mrs. Fry's religious scruples, an appointment was made by the King to meet her at Newgate on the following morning, and afterwards to take luncheon at the house in Upton Lane. This memorable engagement was carried out in its entirety about midday. Mrs. Fry and one of her sisters set out to meet the party, which included the King, his suite, the Lord Mayor and Lady Mayoress, the Sheriffs, some of the Ministers of State, and a large number of gentlemen. The poor women of Newgate numbered about sixty, and doubtless their attention was somewhat distracted by the grand company present ; but Mrs. Fry, with her accustomed common-sense, reminded them that a greater than the King of Prussia was present, even "the King of Kings and Lord of Lords." After this admonition she read the 12th chapter of the Epistle to the Romans, and expounded and conducted a short devotional service. Then, she says, "the King again gave me his arm, and we walked down together. There were difficulties raised about his going to Upton, but he chose to persevere. I went with the Lady Mayoress and the Sheriffs, the King with his own people. We arrived first ; I had to hasten to take off my cloak, and then went down to meet him at his carriage-door, with my husband and seven of our sons and sons-in-law. I then walked with him into the drawing-room, where all was in beautiful order—neat, and adorned with flowers. I presented to the King our eight daughters and daughters-in-law, our seven sons and eldest grandson, my brother and sister Buxton, Sir Henry and Lady Pelley, and my sister-in-law Elizabeth Fry—my brother and sister Gurney he had known before—and afterwards presented twenty-five of our grandchildren. We had a solemn silence before our meal, which was handsome and fit for a king, yet not extravagant, everything most complete and nice. I sat by the King, who appeared to enjoy his dinner, perfectly at his ease and very happy with us. We went into the drawing-room after another silence and a few words which I uttered in prayer for the King and Queen. We found a deputation of Friends with an address to read to him ; this was done ; the King appeared to feel it much. We then had to part. The King expressed his desire that blessings might continue to rest on our house."

Solomon says: " Seest thou a man diligent in his business he shall stand before kings ; he shall not stand before mean men." Elizabeth Fry's life was a living proof of the honors that a persistent, steady, self-denying course of doing good invariably wins in the long run.

CHAPTER XV.

CLOSING DAYS OF LIFE.

INDEFATIGABLE workers wear out, while drones rust out. As the years are counted, of so many days, months, and weeks, many workers of this class die prematurely ; but a wiser philosophy teaches that "He liveth long who liveth well." Into her years of life, long, eventful, and busy, Elizabeth Fry had crowded the work of many ordinary women ; it was little wonder, therefore, that at a time when most people would have settled down to enjoy the relaxations and comforts of a "green old age," she had begun to set her house in order, *to die.* Her energies had been fairly worn out in the service of humanity, and from the time that she made the resolution to serve God, when moved by William Savery's pleadings, right onward through forty-eight years of sunshine and shadow, vicissitudes and labors, she had never swerved from her simple, earnest purpose. The propelling motive to that long course of Christian usefulness may be found in a few words uttered by her shortly before her death : " Since my heart was touched at seventeen years old, I believe I have never awakened from sleep, in sickness or in health, by day or by night, without my first waking thought being, 'how best I might serve my Lord.' " That unchanged desire ultimately became the master-passion of her life.

Honors clustered thickly about her declining days. She was the welcomed guest of royalty and nobility ; on the Continent, as well as in far-away English colonies, her name was pronounced only with respectful love. Her eldest son was appointed to the magistracy of the county ; her relatives and associates were foremost in every enterprise intended to benefit mankind ; while both in Parliament and out of it, her recommendations were respectfully adopted. Had her years been counted on the patriarchal scale, instead of by their own shortened number, she could have reaped no higher honors ; for titles were in her ears but empty sounds, and wealth only meant increased responsibility. Not many nobler souls walked this earth, either in Quaker garb or out of it.

In 1842 her state of health appeared to be so infirm and shattered that her brother-in-law, Mr. Hoare, offered her the loan of his house at Cromer. She accepted the offer for a couple of months, and found a little benefit from the bracing air. She mentioned in her diary at this time that she had "an undue fear of an imbecile or childish state" — a not unlikely feeling to be cherished by an energetic woman accustomed all her life long to the work of helping others. At the end of October she returned home, thankfully rejoicing, however, in an improved state of health.

But a new series of trials awaited her. Death seemed to visit the happy family circle so often that one wonders almost where the tale will stop. Four or five grand-children passed away in rapid succession. After the funeral of the first grand-child, she assembled the family party in the evening, and with a little of the old fire and yearning affection, gave them exhortation and consolation. Then she prayed for all the members of the three generations present. After this funeral service she paid a final visit to France; and then returned home, to descend still further into the valley of suffering.

Her sister-in-law — also named Elizabeth Fry — died during this time of weakness and pain. There had been a close bond of sympathy between these two women; they had travelled many times together as ministers in the Society of Friends, and had been united by the closest bonds of womanly and Christian affection. The faithful sister-in-law preceded the philanthropist to "the better land," by about fifteen months.

In the summer of 1844 she attended her beloved meeting at Plaistow once more. She had been so long in declining health, that meeting with the associates of former years, for worship, had been of necessity an enjoyment altogether out of the question. But Sunday after Sunday, as the "church-going bell" resounded on the still morning air, her spirit yearned to worship God after the manner of her sect. Still, for weeks the attempt was an abortive one. The difficult process of dressing was never accomplished until long after 11 o'clock, the hour when the meeting assembled. The desire was only intensified, however, by these repeated disappointments, and finally it was resolved that the attempt should be made on Sunday, August 4th, at all risks. It succeeded. Drawn by two of her children, in a wheeled chair, she was taken up to the meeting, a few minutes after the hour for commencing worship. Her husband, children and servants followed behind, fearing whether or no the ordeal would be too heavy for the wasted frame. But after remaining for some time in the wonted quiet of the sanctuary, an access of strength seemed to be granted her, and in somewhat similar spirit to that of the old patriarchs, when about to bid fare-

well to the scene of labor and life, she lifted up
her voice once more with weighty, solemn words
of counsel. The prominent topic of her dis-
course was "the death of the righteous." She
expressed the deepest thankfulness, alluding to
her sister-in-law, Elizabeth Fry, for mercies
vouchsafed to one who, having labored amongst
them, had been called from time to eternity.
She quoted that text, "Blessed are the dead
who die in the Lord, for they cease from their
labors, and their works do follow them." She
dwelt on the purposes of affliction, on the utter
weakness and infirmity of the flesh, and then
tenderly exhorted the young. She urged the
need of devotedness of heart and steadfastness
of purpose ; she raised a tribute of praise for the
eternal hope offered to the Christian, and concluded with these words from Isaiah : "Thine
eyes shall see the King in His beauty ; they
shall behold the land that is very far off." Prayer
was afterwards offered by her in a similar strain,
and then the meeting ended. Shortly after
this, a removal to Walmer was effected, in the
vain hope that the footsteps of death might be
retarded.

From one of her letters, written at this date,
we quote the following passage : —

I walk in a low valley, still I believe I may say that the
everlasting arms are underneath me, and the Lord is very

near. I pass through deep waters, but I trust, as my Lord is near to me, they will not overflow me. I need all your prayers in my low estate. I think the death of my sister, and dear little Gurney, has been almost too much for me.

But Mrs. Fry was to pass through still deeper waters of affliction and trial while in her suffering state. A visitation of scarlet fever attacked the family of her son William, and, in spite of all medical attentions, he and two of his daughters fell beneath the destroyer's hand. A scene of desolation ensued; the servants, as they sickened, were taken to Guy's Hospital, and the Manor House was deserted, for those members of the household who had escaped the infection had to flee for their lives. For a time, the dear ones who ministered to Mrs. Fry were too terror-stricken and crushed by the trial to venture on telling their mother all; more than that, they feared for her life also. But the "Christian's faith proved stronger than the mother's anguish. She wept abundantly, almost unceasingly; but she dwelt constantly on the unseen world, seeking for passages in the Bible which speak of the happy state of the righteous. She was enabled to rejoice in the rest upon which her beloved ones had entered, and in a wonderful manner to realize the blessedness of their lot." Her other children gathered around her at Walmer, anxious to comfort her, and be themselves comforted by her in this succession of bereavements. She had been such a tower of strength to all her family, in the years which had gone, that they almost instinctively clustered around her now with the old trustful, yearning devotion; but she was, although firm in spirit, so frail in body as to be like the trembling ivy requiring the most constant and tender support. Writing in her journal about this time, Mrs. Fry thus expressed her feelings: "Sorrow upon sorrow! The trial is almost inexpressible. Oh! dear Lord, keep thy unworthy servant in this time of severe trial; keep me sound in faith and clear in mind, and be very near to us all." Shortly after this entry a beloved niece died; and, as if the hungry maw of Death were not yet satisfied, Sir Thomas Fowell Buxton, her brother-in-law, friend and coadjutor in so many benevolent schemes, also became a victim. It is certain that these numerous losses weaned her much from life; it is also certain that her splendid reasoning powers gave way for a time, and the infirmity of premature old age crept over her mind. In this way she was mercifully kept from being utterly crushed. Yet, while her mental strength remained, she thought lovingly of those ladies who had been associated with her in her philanthropic works and penned a few lines of parting counsel to them. The following is the text of the last written communication addressed by her to the Committee of the Ladies' British Society :—

My much-loved friends, amidst many sorrows that have been permitted for me to pass through, and much bodily suffering, I still feel a deep and lively interest in the cause of poor prisoners; and earnest is my prayer that the God of all grace may be very near to help you to be steadfast in the important Christian work of seek-ing to win the poor wanderers to return, repent and live; that they may know Christ to be their Saviour, Redeemer and hope of glory. May the Holy Spirit direct your steps, strengthen your hearts, and enable you and me to glorify our Holy Head in doing and suffering even unto the end; and when the end comes, through a Saviour's love and merits, may we be received into glory and everlasting rest and peace.

In the spring of 1845 she paid a last visit to Earlham Hall. She had, with the tenacity of desire peculiar to invalids, longed intensely to behold again the scenes amid which her youth was spent, and to welcome once more those familiar faces yet left in the old home. While there she was several times drawn to the meet-ing at Norwich, and even spoke on different occasions with her wonted fire and persuasive-ness. It seemed as if her powerful memory was revived, seeing that the stores of Scripture which she had made hers were now drawn upon with singular aptness and felicity. After paying one or two farewell visits to North Repps and Runcton she returned once more to Upton Lane. Once settled there, she received many marks of sympathy from the excellent of all denominations, as well as from the noble and rich. The Duchess of Sutherland and her daughters, the Chevalier de Bunsen, and others who had heard of or known her, called upon her with every token of respectful affection ; while, on her part, she spoke and acted as if in the very light of Eternity. So anxious, indeed, was she still to do what she conceived to be her Master's work, that she made prodigious efforts to attend meetings connected with the Society of Friends and with her own special prison work. Thus she was present at two of the yearly meetings for Friends in London in May, and on June 3d attended the annual meeting at the British Ladies' Society. This meeting was removed from the usual place at Westminster to the Friends' meeting-house at Plaistow, in deference to Mrs. Fry's infirm health and visibly-declining strength. In a report issued by this society, some four or five weeks after Mrs. Fry's death, the committee paid a fitting tribute to her labors with them, and the sacred preëminence she had won in the course of those labors. In the memorial they referred to this meeting in the following terms:—

Contrary to usual custom, the place of meeting fixed on was not in London, but at Plaistow, in Essex, and the large number of friends who gathered around her on that occasion, proved how gladly they came to her when she could no longer, with ease, be conveyed to them. The enfeebled state of her bodily frame seemed to have left the powers of her mind unshackled, and she took, though in a sitting posture, almost her usual part in repeatedly addressing the meeting. She urged, with increased pathos and affection, the objects of philanthropy and Christian benevolence with which her life had been identified. After the meeting, and at her own desire, several members of the committee, and other friends, assembled at her house. They were welcomed by her with the greatest benignity and kindness, and in her intercourse with them, strong were the indications of the heavenly teaching through which her subdued and sanctified spirit had been called to pass. Her affectionate salutation in parting, unconsciously closed, in regard to most of them, the intercourse which they delighted to hold with her, but which can be no more renewed on this side of the eternal world.

At this time Mrs. Fry found intense satisfaction in learning that the London prisons — Newgate, Bridewell, Millbank, Giltspur Street Compter, Whitecross Street, Tothill Fields, and Coldbath Fields — were all in more or less excellent order, and regularly visited by the ladies who had been her coadjutors, and were to be her successors.

A few weeks later she was taken to Ramsgate, in the hope that the sea-air would restore her strength for a little time ; and while there her old interest in the Coastguard Libraries returned, fresh and lively as ever. It was, indeed, a proof of the ruling passion being strong in almost dying circumstances. She attended meeting whenever possible, obtained a grant of Bibles and Testaments from the Bible Society, arranged, sorted, and distributed them among the sailors in the harbor, with the help of her grandchildren, and manifested, by her daily deportment, how fully she had learned the hard lesson of submission and patience in suffering.

A few days before the end, pressure of the brain became apparent ; severe pain, succeeded by torpor and loss of power, and, after a short time, utter unconsciousness, proved that the sands of life had nearly run down. A few hours of spasmodic suffering followed, very trying to those who watched by ; but suddenly, about four on the morning of October 13th, 1845, the silver cord was loosed, the pitcher broken at the fountain, and the spirit returned to God who gave it.

In a quiet grave at Barking, by the side of the little child whom she had loved and lost, years before, rest Elizabeth Fry's mortal remains. "God buries His workers, but carries on His work." The peculiar work which made her name and life so famous has grown and ripened right up to the present hour. In this, "her name liveth for evermore."

CHAPTER XVI.

SINCE the days when John Howard, Elizabeth Fry and other prison reformers first commenced to grapple with the great problems of how to treat criminals, many, animated by the purest motives, have followed in the same path. To Captain Maconochie, perhaps, is due the system of rewards awarded to convicts who manifest a desire to amend, and show by their exemplary conduct that they are anxious to regain once more a fair position in society. Some anonymous writers have recently treated the public to books bearing on the convict system of our country; and professedly written, as they are, by men who have endured longer or shorter periods of penal servitude, their opinions and suggestions certainly count for something. The author of *Five Years' Penal Servitude* seems to entertain very decided opinions upon the present system and its faults. He speaks strongly against *long* sentences for first offences, but urges that they should be made more severe.

He thinks that short sentences, made as severe as possible, consistent with safety to life, would act as a deterrent more effectually than the long punishments, which are, to a certain degree, mild to all well-conducted prisoners. He also most strongly advocates separation of prisoners; insisting that "the mixing of prisoners together is radically bad, and should at all costs be done away with. Men who are imprisoned for first offences, whether it be in a county jail or a convict prison, should most certainly be kept perfectly distinct from 'second-timers,' and not on any account be brought into contact with old offenders, who, in too many cases, simply complete their education in vice." He further states, in a concise form, what, in his estimation, should be the aim of all penal measures. 1st. The punishment of those who have transgressed the laws of the country, and the deterring others from crime; 2d. The getting rid of the troublesome and criminal class of the population; 3d. The doing of this in the most efficient and least costly way to the tax-paying British public. He even quotes the opinion that New Guinea would be suitable as a place of disposal for the convict class. But many and good reasons have been given against shipping off criminals to be pests to other people; this system has been already tried, and failed to a

large extent, although it certainly had redeem-
ing features. Looking at the matter all round,
it seems utterly impossible to devise a convict
system which shall meet fairly and justly all
cases. Could some system be set in operation
which should afford opportunity for the thought-
less and unwary criminal, who has heedlessly
fallen into temptation, to retrace his steps and
attain once more the height whence he has
fallen, it would be a boon to society. On the
other hand, the members of the really criminal
class only anticipate liberty in order to use it
for fresh crime, for, in their opinion, the shame
lies in detection, not in sinning. What can
be done with such but to deal stringently with
them as with enemies against society? This
writer can fully bear out Mrs. Fry's emphatic
recommendations as to the imperative necessity
that exists for complete separation and classification of the prisoners, in all our penal estab-
lishments. Association of the prisoners, one
with another, only carries on and completes
their criminal and vicious education.

There is, however, a general *consensus* of
opinion as to the desirability of reformatory,
rather than punitive measures, being dealt out to
children and very young persons. This system
has, in almost every case, been found to work
well. The authors of *The Jail Cradle, Who*

Rocks It? and *In Prison and Out,* have dealt with the problem of juvenile crime—and not in vain. From the latter work, the following paragraph proves that in this matter, as in many others, Germany is abreast of the age :—

In Germany, no child under twelve years of age can suffer a penal sentence. Between twelve and eighteen years of age, youthful criminals are free to declare whether, while committing the offense, they were fully aware of their culpability against the laws of their country. In every case, every term of imprisonment above one month is carried out, not in a jail, but in an institution specially set apart and adapted for old offenders. These institutions serve not only for the purpose of punishment, but also provide for the education of the prisoners, *the neglect of education being recognized as one of the chief sources of crime.*

Mrs. Fry dealt with women principally, and it was only in a very limited degree that she could benefit the children of these fallen ones. Still there can be no doubt that she did a large service to society in taking possession of them and educating them while with their mothers. What that work involved has been fully told in the preceding pages ; its results no pen can compute. Woman-like, she aimed at the improvement of her own sex; but the reform which she inaugurated did not stop there. Like a circle caused by the descent of a pebble into a lake, it widened and extended and spread until

she and her work became household words
among all classes of society, and in all civilized
countries. Most women would have shrunk
back appalled at the terrible scene of degradation which Newgate presented when she first
entered its wards as a visitor ; others would
have deemed it impossible to accomplish anything, save under the auspices of Government,
and by the aid of public funds. Not thus did
she regard the matter, but with earnest, oft-re-
peated endeavors, she set herself to stem the
tide of sin and suffering to be found at that
period in Government jails, and so successfully
that a radical change passed over the whole
system before she died. Probably it is not too
much to say that no laborer in the cause of
prison reform ever won a larger share of success.
Certainly none ever received a larger meed of
reverential love.